THE BULL IN THE GARDEN

THE BULL
IN THE
GARDEN

A History of Allston-Brighton

by William P. Marchione

Boston, Trustees of the Public Library
of the City of Boston, 1986

Dedicated to The Brighton Historical Society

Credits

To the Society for the Preservation of New England Antiquities
for illustrations in Chapters VI, VII, VIII; to the *Allston-
Brighton Item* for the illustration in Chapter X; to the Brighton
Historical Society for other illustrations.

For the map of Allston-Brighton included at the end of this
publication special acknowledgment is extended to Harry D. Lord
& Son, Map Publishers, Framingham, Massachusetts.

Library of Congress Cataloging-in-Publications Data

Marchione, William P., 1942–
  The bull in the garden.

  Includes index.
  1. Allston (Boston, Mass.)—History. 2. Brighton (Boston,
Mass.)—History. 3. Boston (Mass.)—History. I. Title.
F73.68.A44M37 1986   974.4'61   86-6944
ISBN 0-89073-078-4

Designed by Richard Zonghi

Edited by Jane Manthorne

Contents

Introduction

Publication of *The Bull in the Garden* marks the attainment of a goal I set for myself over twenty-five years ago, when, as a high school student, I realized that no general history of Allston-Brighton existed and promised myself that I would someday write one. The only previous full-length work on the subject, J.C.P. Winship's turn-of-the-century *Historical Brighton*, a compendium of genealogical sketches, while a goldmine of information is extremely confusing for the contemporary reader. It was only in 1976, however, when I became chairman of the Brighton Historical Society's research committee, that I began addressing the task of producing a history.

If there had been no Brighton Historical Society, it is unlikely that this book would exist. Several of its chapters were written expressly for the Society—as programs for its quarterly meetings or as articles for its publications. The first draft of *The Bull in the Garden* was prepared for a lecture series given under Society auspices in the spring of 1982. Thus the dedication of this book to the organization that has consistently nourished my work with its interest, support, and applause. A special debt of gratitude is owed the hearty band that joined me in so many research projects, the members of the BHS research committee: Raymond McCarron, Brian McLaughlin, Walter Prussman, Aurora Salvucci, and Charles Vasiliades.

For reading and criticizing portions of the manuscript

and for calling it to the attention of the Trustees of the Boston Public Library, I am deeply grateful to Professor Andrew Buni of Boston College. Special thanks also to Edythe York and Patricia O'Brien for their assistance in preparing the manuscript. Finally, I would like to thank my wife, Mary Ann, and our children, David and Karen, for their patience and understanding of my long-term obsession with Allston-Brighton history.

The choice of the title *The Bull in the Garden* requires some explanation. It has both a literal and figurative meaning. Its application to the 19th century is, I think, fairly obvious, for cattle and horticulture then dominated the local scene. But the title has relevance for our time as well. It refers to unregulated development, which today more than ever threatens Allston-Brighton's environment, the quality of its life, our "garden."

William P. Marchione

Allston-Brighton
April 19, 1986

CHAPTER I

Establishing Little Cambridge

1630–1690

In 1629 Reverend Francis Higginson, as agent of the Massachusetts Bay Company, explored the area with which this history is concerned.

> It is a land of diverse and sundry sorts all about Massachusetts Bay [he wrote home to London], and at Charles River is as fat black earth as can be seen anywhere.

> Though all the country be as it were a thick wood for the general, yet in diverse places there is much ground cleared by the Indians . . . and I am told that about three miles from us a man may stand on a little hilly place and see diverse thousands of acres of ground as good as need to be, and not a tree in the same.[1]

The Charles River Valley had once been the home of a large Indian population. Its hills, streams, and ponds provided excellent sites for summer encampments. Its waters teemed with fish. Moose, caribou, beaver, otter, lynx, turkeys, geese, and cranes roamed the surrounding woods. Corn, beans, squash, pumpkins, and cucumbers grew abundantly in its fertile soil.

In 1616 and 1617, however, plague devastated the Indians of the region. Whole villages were wiped out by

1

this disease, whole territories abandoned. As historian Alden Vaughan noted: "this largely accounts for the cordiality with which the [Massachusetts] tribe received the Puritan immigrants, for any friendly neighbors, particularly if equipped with firearms, were a valuable shield against possible extermination."[2]

English settlement on the Charles River began in 1630 with the foundation of three towns: Boston, Watertown, and Cambridge. Initially, the land comprising Allston-Brighton was assigned to Watertown. Watertown Minister George Philips received the first grant of land in Allston-Brighton in 1630, 30 acres on the river near the present Brighton-Newton boundary. Still, the presence of Indians on the south side of the Charles discouraged settlement there for some years.[3]

In 1634 the General Court of the Massachusetts Bay Colony transferred ownership of the "south side of the river" to Cambridge, a town which suffered from a shortage of grazing land. The area was used for grazing as early as 1635, when Cambridge contracted with William Patten "to keep 100 cattle on the other side of the river for the space of seven months" for 20 pounds. "He is to lodge there except once a week," the agreement continued, "and to have a man to keep them every other sabbath day." Patten, in turn, agreed to pay the town ten shillings "for every beast he shall lose; and to keep no cattle of any man, except the Townsmen give leave, upon forefeiture of five shillings a head for every head he shall so keep."[4]

The Charles River of the colonial era was a tidal estuary bordered by hundreds of acres of salt marshes. Anyone living on the river's southern shore would be both isolated and vulnerable to Indian attack. Cambridge began granting south side land as early as 1635; but the first family to establish itself within the boundaries of Allston-Brighton, the Holleys, did not settle until 1639, and stayed only temporarily.

Samuel Holley, the first resident of Allston-Brighton, came to the south side with the group that established Cambridge Village (Newton) in 1639. His 18-acre estate stood west of Oak Square on Washington Hill. On his death in 1643, the property passed into the hands of his wife Elizabeth and an unnamed son. Elizabeth's second husband, John Kendall, sold the property to Newton neighbor Edward Jackson in 1646.[5]

Permanent settlement in Allston-Brighton dates from the 1647–49 period. Rev. John Eliot's conversion of the local natives to the Christian religion removed a major obstacle to the establishment of homesteads on the south side of the Charles.

A small band of Indians under the leadership of Waban had lived in the vicinity of Nonantum Hill for some time. Prior attempts to convert the Massachusetts Bay Indians to Christianity having failed, Eliot decided to proselytize Waban, whom he described as "one who gives more grounded hope of serious respect for the things of God, than any as yet I have known of that forlorne generation."[6] The English knew Waban as "The Merchant." It was in order to be closer to the white settlements that he moved to the vicinity from his native Concord. His son was attending an English school in Dedham. In Waban Eliot found an Indian leader eager to be assimilated by the English.

Accompanying Eliot to Waban's encampment were three companions, Thomas Shepard, Minister of Cambridge; Daniel Gookin, afterwards Supervisor of Indian towns for the Massachusetts Bay Colony; and either John Wilson, Minister of Boston, or Elder Heath of Roxbury (on this point the record is unclear). Waban's encampment consisted of a few wigwams enclosed by a stockade. Eliot did his preaching outside of Waban's hut, the largest dwelling in the village, which stood central and a little apart from the others. A small company of Indian

Reverend John Eliot, New England's great Indian missionary, began his campaign for Christianity with a sermon on Nonantum Hill in October 1646.

men, women, and children had arranged themselves on the ground in front of this structure, with their blankets drawn tightly around them. Some of the men leaned against trees a bit further off, almost out of hearing.

The date was October 18, 1646. This hour-long sermon in the Algonquian language initiated Eliot's long crusade for the souls of the Massachusetts Bay natives—a crusade

4

that led to the establishment of fourteen Christian Indian communities in the thirty years that followed.

As his guests were leaving, recounted Rev. Thomas Shepard, Waban approached and said, "We need more ground to build our town on."

"I will speak to the General Court about that," Eliot answered.[7]

On November 4, 1646, the General Court of the Massachusetts Bay Colony voted to grant the desired land "for the good of the Indians" and appointed a commission to attend to the matter, which included Eliot. When the Indians inquired what name to give their Christian village, Eliot wrote, "It was told them it should be called Nonantum, which signifies in English rejoicing, because they hearing the word, and seeking to know God, the English did rejoice at it."[8]

An early historian of Newton, the Rev. Jonathan Homer, has left us the following description of the "Praying Indian" village of Nonantum.

Mr. Eliot . . . furnished them, by the public aid, with shovels, spades, mattocks, and iron crows, and stimulated the most industrious with money; they soon built a sufficient number of wigwams, not with mats as usual, but with the bark of trees, and divided into several distinct apartments. The houses of the meanest were found to be equal to those of the sachems or chiefs in other places. They surrounded the town with ditches . . . and with a stone-wall.

The Indians, thus settled, were instructed in husbandry, and were excited to a prudent as well as industrious management of their affairs. Some of them were taught such trades as were most necessary for them, so that they completely built a house for public worship, 50 feet in length and 25 feet in breadth.

The women of Nonantum soon learnt to spin, and to collect for sale at the market through the year. In the winter, the Indians sold brooms, staves, baskets, made from neighboring woods and swamps, and turkies raised by themselves; in the spring, cranberries, strawberries, and fish from Charles River; in the summer whortleberries, grapes, and fish. Several of them worked with the English in the vicinity, in haytime and harvest.[9]

Nonantum's population grew so rapidly that the community soon ran out of land. Thus in 1651 Eliot was obliged to move the entire population some fifteen miles to the southwest, to a 3,000-acre site in the present town of Natick.

The area had not, however, seen the last of the Praying Indians. In 1676, during King Philip's War, the bloodiest of New England's Indian conflicts, the General Court ordered the internment of the Praying Indians on Deer Island in Boston Harbor "for their own protection."[10] The Natick Indians were accordingly marched to "The Pines" on the Charles River (the Soldier's Field Road Extension crosses the site today), where three large boats waited to transport them to their harbor prison. At the end of 1676 the survivors were permitted to return to Natick, the Pines serving as the point of disembarkation. Deacon Thomas Oliver, a prominent local citizen, allowed the natives to camp on his land near Brooks Street during the return trip.[11]

Despite Cambridge's easterly location, it would be a mistake to assume that the community did not feel the effects of this war. At least six Little Cambridge residents served in the Middlesex Regiment commanded by Captain Daniel Gookin, Indian Commissioner of Massachusetts in the 1660s and 1670s: Thomas Brown, Samuel Champney, Thomas Oliver, Samuel Robbins, John Smith, and John

6

Squire. Moreover, the danger of an Indian attack upon Cambridge was serious enough to warrant the construction of a stockade around the town. According to Paige, "the stockade was commenced" in the spring of 1676, "but before it was completed the danger so far diminished that the project was abandoned, and the timber which had been gathered was used to repair the Great Bridge."[12] It is possible that the Indian peril led to the temporary removal of some Little Cambridge families to the relative safety of Cambridge proper.

In June 1647, less than a year after Eliot visited Waban, Richard and Susannah Champney moved to a 149-acre tract on the south side of the Charles, just east of the present Union Square. The history of Allston-Brighton as a distinct community (called Little Cambridge before 1807) begins with this event.

Richard Champney, who emigrated from Lincolnshire, England in 1635, was an important figure in early Cambridge. Religion played a central role in the lives of the Puritan founders of Massachusetts. As Ruling Elder of the Cambridge Church, Champney occupied a position second only to the minister as a church leader. Rev. Thomas Shepard described Elder Champney as a "most dear saint."[13] As Cotton Mather wrote, Champney's responsibilities included "assist[ing] the pastor in visiting the distressed, instructing the ignorant, reducing the erroneous, comforting the afflicted, rebuking the unruly, discovering the state of the whole flock, exercising the discipline of the Gospel upon offenders, and promoting the desirable growth of the church."[14]

Little Cambridge's next settler, Richard Dana, emigrated from Manchester, England in 1640. In 1647 Cambridge granted him a mile-long tract of land extending west from the Pines. He moved to this property in 1647 following his marriage to Anne Bullard of Watertown. In subsequent generations, the family they founded produced many notable statesmen, diplomats, jurists, and authors.

Richard and Anne Dana built three houses in Little Cambridge. Their first residence stood just east of the present Faneuil and Brooks Street intersection. In 1658, however, they sold this dwelling and 58 acres of land to Edward Jackson of Newton, and moved to a second homestead nearer the Pines, on the site of the present Faneuil Housing Project.

A second move came in 1661, when the Danas acquired a 108-acre estate on the western end of Little Cambridge, south of Oak Square, a property that extended over Nonantum Hill into the present Chandler's Pond area. Their third residence, which remained in the family well into the second half of the nineteenth century, stood at the northeast corner of Nonantum and Washington Streets. It was here, in 1690, that the aged Richard Dana died in a fall from a scaffold.[15]

Nathaniel Sparhawk II settled in Little Cambridge in 1649, following his marriage to Patience Newman, daughter of the Minister of Rehoboth, Massachusetts. The Sparhawk family had emigrated from Dedham, England in 1636. Nathaniel I, who represented Cambridge in the General Court for many years, was a man of considerable wealth and influence. At the time of his death in 1647, his estate included five houses and over a thousand acres of land. Nathaniel II inherited the bulk of this property, including much Little Cambridge acreage. The Sparhawk estate was situated east of Market Street. The homestead stood near the present Sparhawk and Market Streets intersection.[16]

While these three families—the Champneys, Danas and Sparhawks—are traditionally referred to as the founders of Little Cambridge, others quickly followed.

In the early 1650s John Oldham settled on a 90-acre property south of Faneuil Street. When he died in 1655, the estate went to his widow Martha and two sons, Samuel and John. In 1656 Martha married Thomas Brown, who purchased the estate and built the house on Faneuil Street that was afterwards known as the Parsons Mansion. Thomas Cheney purchased the second Dana house and 70-acres of land in 1661. In 1670 Thomas Oliver, a stepson of Edward Jackson of Newton, acquired the original Dana homestead, a property afterwards known as the Brooks Estate. Oliver was an important political figure in colonial Massachusetts who held the office of Governor's Councillor at the time of his death in 1715.

Other early settlers included the Smith brothers, Henry and John, who owned considerable acreage south of what is now Brighton Center, and Nathaniel Robbins, whose estate, the most remote in Little Cambridge, was situated near the present Chestnut Hill Reservoir.[17]

The Pines was the focal point of early settlement in Little Cambridge. This spot on the tidal Charles, with its high banks, offered the most reliable crossing point in the area.[18] In 1633, years before south side settlement began, the General Court established a ferry between Watertown and the Pines. The order read, "Richard Brown is allowed to keep a ferry over Charles River against his house and is to have two pence for every single person he so transports and one penny apiece if there be two or more." The residents of Little Cambridge used this ferry when travelling to church and to the seat of local government in the present Harvard Square.[19]

The local water supply also influenced the location of early homesteads. A major brook, referred to in the early records as Dana Brook, ran through the Dana Estate. Its source lay in the valleys formed by Waban, Nonantum, and Washington Hills. The streams flowing out of those valleys converged near the present Faneuil Square before emptying into the Charles River in the vicinity of the Pines. A second major brook crossed the Sparhawk Estate.

Its source lay in the vicinity of the present Wallingford Road. This brook meandered across the Sparhawk property before emptying into the Charles River in North Allston.[20]

An Old Indian path running west from the pines served Little Cambridge as its first roadway. A portion of that path still survives as Nonantum Street. In 1656 the Selectmen of Cambridge replaced the eastern part of the path with two roads, the present Market and Faneuil Streets. Market Street, which was laid out along the boundary of the Sparhawk and Dana property, converged with a road which the towns of Boston, Cambridge, and Watertown were constructing from the Muddy River to the Watertown Mill (the present Washington Street). Faneuil Street, which curved around the edge of high land, paralleled the old Indian path, which was too close to the river to be convenient in all seasons.[21]

Another important local roadway was the Roxbury Highway, which passed through the eastern section of Little Cambridge. This road, established in 1638, linked Cambridge directly to Boston. It must be remembered that the Back Bay was then quite literally a bay—a barrier to direct communication with the colony's largest town and seat of government. The Roxbury Highway ran from the village of Cambridge to the river, where a ferry had been operating since 1634. In December, 1635, the General Court ordered "that there shall be a sufficient bridge [over the salt marsh] made down to low-water mark on this side of the river [the north side] and a broad ladder [set up] on the farther side of the river for convenience [of] landing, and Mr. Chaplin, Mr. Danforth, and Mr. Cooke to see to it." The ferry toll here was half that of the Pines, reflecting the heavier traffic utilizing the Roxbury Highway.[22] The Highway then followed the line of the present North Harvard, Cambridge, and Harvard Streets across Allston and Brookline and over the "neck" into Boston, thereby skirting the Back Bay in a great eight mile arc.[23]

In 1663 the colonial government decided to replace the ferry, largely useless in winter and inconvenient for the transportation of carts and livestock, with The Great Bridge, the largest such structure in the colony. The Great Bridge proved difficult to build and even more difficult to maintain. The original structure, supported by hollow logs filled with stones, was swept away by a flood in 1685. In 1690 the bridge was rebuilt on piles, a difficult construction technique since only hand power was available for raising the weight of the driver. Tradition tells us that five thousand blows were required to drive some of the piles to firm bearing. Since the cost of maintaining the bridge was high, the colony at first resorted to charging tolls. Later, however, it devised a formula for public maintenance of the structure: one-half to be borne by Middlesex County, one-third by Cambridge, and one-sixth by the newly incorporated town of Newton.[24]

With the withdrawal of Newton from Cambridge in 1688, Little Cambridge became the only part of Cambridge south of the Charles River.

Little Cambridge had grown slowly. In 1688 it contained just twenty-seven households, a population too sparse to support an independent church or town government. As its numbers grew in the century that followed, however, the south-side community would seek an increased degree of local self-determination.[25]

CHAPTER II

Steps Toward Independence
1690–1790

Little Cambridge remained a sparsely settled agricultural community in the 18th century. Its population rose only slightly, from 125 to 350, between 1690 and 1790. Though it contained less than 20 percent of Cambridge's total population, the south-side community was well represented in the government of the town with at least one selectman's position going to a Little Cambridge resident in town elections throughout the period. Cambridge's seat in the colonial legislature was also frequently filled from Little Cambridge. A handful of prominent families monopolized these positions—the Sparhawks, Danas, Champneys, and Oldhams exclusively before 1769.[1]

The Town of Cambridge occupied a special place in the life of Colonial New England. As historian S. B. Sutton noted, "insofar as there was an intellectual center in the colonies it [had] existed unchallenged in Cambridge during the seventeenth century. For many decades thereafter, Harvard supplied New England with teachers and ministers, thereby putting its moral stamp on the new world spreading into the wilderness."[2]

Apart from the college, however, Cambridge was a fairly typical eastern Massachusetts farming community. Boston and other nearby population centers provided markets for the products of its farms and fields, particularly its cattle, dairy products, and fruit. Large sections of the town—including much of present-day Allston—were utilized for

12

grazing. Reflecting the high degree of economic vitality was an extensive reliance upon indentured servants and slaves. Of the 58 families residing in Little Cambridge in 1777, eight were slaveowners, blacks then making up about 5 percent of the community's population. The slaveowners included such prominent families as the Sparhawks, Faneuils, Winships, and Gardners. Slavery was not abolished in Massachusetts until 1781.[3]

As time went on a large number of wealthy families established residences in Cambridge. The Vassalls, Inmans, Phipses, Lechmeres, and Faneuils built their fortunes in the mercantile trade of the port city, but preferred the open fields and pleasant gardens of Cambridge to cramped, noisy, unhealthy Boston. Most built elaborate Georgian style residences on the road to Watertown [Brattle Street]. An exception was Benjamin Faneuil, who in 1760 purchased an estate at the western end of Little Cambridge.

As late as the mid-1700s, Cambridge was still heavily wooded. A Harvard student wrote in 1759: "A great many bears killed at Cambridge and the surrounding towns about this time, and several persons killed by them." While healthier than Boston, even rural Cambridge suffered deadly epidemics from time to time. An outbreak in 1730 led to the dismissal of the college; in June 1740 an epidemic of throat distemper caused many deaths.[4]

While the political union with Cambridge continued into the 19th century, Little Cambridge's first step toward local self-determination was taken in 1722, when the residents established a schoolhouse near the northeast corner of Market and Washington Streets on land furnished by Daniel Dana, the youngest son of Richard Dana. It was here that Little Cambridge residents gathered to conduct public business prior to the establishment of a local meetinghouse.[5] This was not a free school. Though the Town of Cambridge maintained it out of general revenues and the local population selected a committee to manage the facility, in 1720 "each child" was ordered to "pay Ten Shillings Old Tenor at his or her entrance into the school."[6] A larger schoolhouse was built at the same location in 1769, the old one having proven "insufficient to contain the scholars, and not worth repairing."[7] The original building must have been tiny indeed, for the new one measured a meager 28 by 20 feet. It was described as "ruff boarded within and filled with brick and clay and clapboard outside, with a proper chimney, windows, desk and seats and finished in a neat and plain manner."[8]

Another step toward independence was taken in 1734 when the community successfully petitioned the colonial legislature for permission to hold religious services in Little Cambridge in winter. George B. Livermore, historian of the First Church of Brighton, noted that the petitioners had "no idea of separation from the parent church . . . at that time: they expected to meet with their old associates when practicable, and probably any suggestion of complete alienation and independent action would have been condemned as worse than heresy, and stamped out as rebellion." The earliest meetinghouse in Little Cambridge was described only as a deserted farmhouse.[9] "It is supposed to have been located at the southwest corner of Cambridge and North Harvard Street," Winship wrote.[10]

In 1738 a committee of local residents recommended the construction of a meetinghouse at the northeast corner of Washington and Market Streets, adjacent to the school-house. Such a structure would cost £ 380, the committee reported, recommending that sum be raised by sub-scription. It was not until 1744, however, that the proposed structure was built.[11] The largest subscriber to the meetinghouse fund was Captain Nathaniel Cunning-ham, who resided in a large mansion on the site now occupied by St. Gabriel's Monastery, an estate an early map identifies as "Captain Cunningham's Seat."

14

The Little Cambridge Meetinghouse, it should be emphasized, was merely an annex or chapel of the First Church of Cambridge. While its members no longer worshipped at the parent church in Harvard Square, they were technically still members of the old church and therefore obligated to pay for its upkeep. This double payment system, which prevailed for nearly forty years, vexed the people of Little Cambridge.

The struggle to win independent status for the Little Cambridge Church began in 1747. It was not finally won, however, until 1783. The people of Little Cambridge regularly petitioned the colonial legislature or General Court throughout the period. According to the 1749 petititon, Little Cambridge contained 2,660 acres, 42 dwelling houses, 50 families, 290 residents, and paid £700 in Provincial taxes. Fifty of its residents were "in full communion with the church." Here was a community, the petition asserted, fully capable of supporting its own church.[12]

The General Court rejected these petitions for two reasons. The middle 18th century was a period of intense religious controversy in Massachusetts. Anything that threatened to weaken the religious establishment was regarded with deep suspicion. In addition, three prominent Little Cambridge families—the Gardners, Griggses, and the family of Samuel Sparhawk—actively opposed separation. Since these families lived in the northern part of Little Cambridge, they found it more convenient to worship at the old church in Harvard Square. The Griggs and Gardner estates were situated on the lower Roxbury Highway (near the present Allston business district). Samuel Sparhawk resided on Western Avenue.

A petition dated January 26, 1774 complained that the Minister of Cambridge, Dr. Nathan Appleton, who was 81 years old at the time, was physically unable to attend to the needs of Little Cambridge.

15

We have been put to much difficulty to get an ordained minister to baptise our children; and have
never had the ordinance of the Lord's Supper
amongst us, and we apprehend that many of our
children, that are arrived at man's estate, have never
seen the ordinance administered. Many times, when
our friends are upon their death-beds, they have no
minister either to pray with them, or afford them any
advice or instruction in their dying moments. We are
also deprived of having a discrete minister to set an
example before, and instruct our children in the
knowledge that is necessary to eternal salvation.[13]

To correct this injustice, the south-side parishioners
proposed that two ministers be settled at Cambridge, with
one assigned to serve their community.

The General Court finally approved the separation of
the churches in April 1779, thirty-two years after the
original petition was submitted. It is probably no accident
that permission came during the Revolution when Massachusetts conservatism was relatively weak. The enabling
act contained a clause specifically exempting "Samuel
Sparhawk, John Gardner, Moses Griggs, and their present
estates . . . from all ministerial taxes to said south precinct
so long as they shall live." According to Cambridge
historian Lucius Paige, the Little Cambridge congregation
petitioned the First Church of Cambridge for official
dismissal in 1780. "The church," Paige wrote, "voted a
compliance with their petition; and they were incorporated on the 23rd of February, 1783. The Reverend John
Foster was ordained to their pastoral charge, November 4,
1784."[14]

With church services now being held year round in
Little Cambridge, the inconvenient practice of burying the
dead in the old First Church Burial Ground in Harvard
Square was discontinued. The congregation purchased a

16

half-acre parcel of land to the rear of the Meetinghouse from Nathaniel Sparhawk in 1764. This small cemetery, the Market Street Burial Ground, served the community until 1850.[15]

As noted previously, the founding families of Little Cambridge, the Champneys, Danas, and Sparhawks, dominated public office for much of the 18th century. The election of Thomas Gardner to the posts of Selectman and Representative to the General Court in 1769 broke this pattern.

Gardner was born in 1723, probably in Brookline. The details of his upbringing and education are unknown. The Gardner family was fairly wealthy.[16] In 1747 Thomas' father, Richard Gardner, purchased a 110-acre estate on the lower Roxbury Highway, paying more than £ 3,000 for the property. The Gardner house stood at the northwest corner of Harvard and Brighton Avenues. The structure was moved to nearby Higgins Street in 1850, and is still standing. It is the oldest house in Allston.

Thomas Gardner was twenty-four years old in 1747, unmarried, and as the oldest son, stood to inherit the bulk of his father's estate. His marriage to Joanna Sparhawk in 1755 allied him to one of Little Cambridge's wealthiest families. That alliance was strengthened in 1757 when his sister Elizabeth married Joanna's oldest brother, Thomas Sparhawk. [17]

Gardner's career in public life was brief, spanning just six years. He wielded considerable influence in the affairs of Massachusetts, however, particularly in the year leading to the outbreak of the Revolution.[18] When the King dissolved the General Court in 1774, following the Boston Tea Party, Gardner was in the forefront of those urging resistance. He was chosen to represent Cambridge in the Middlesex County Convention called to consider measures for the public safety, as well as in the First and Second Provincial Congresses. A military expert, Gardner served on committees of defense and public safety.

Gardner was a fervent revolutionary. When loyalist Chief Justice Peter Oliver refused to vacate his judicial post in defiance of an order of the Massachusetts House of Deputies, Gardner threatened to personally drag the offending jurist from the bench. "We trust the day is not far distant," he declared in early 1775, "when our rights shall be returned to us, or the colonies united as one man, will make their most solemn appeal to heaven, and drive tyranny from these northern shores."[19]

Gardner's growing prominence in the affairs of revolutionary Massachusetts was evidenced by his election in May 1775 to the Revolutionary Council of Safety, the body that replaced the Royal Governor and Council as the executive branch of the Massachusetts government. The defense of Massachusetts was of more pressing concern, however. In the spring of 1775, he was commissioned a colonel of a regiment he had organized largely at his own expense.

Gardner's meteoric rise to political and military prominence ended tragically at the Battle of Bunker Hill in June 1775. Richard Frothingham provided the following detailed account of the circumstances of Gardner's death in his classic *History of the Siege of Boston:*

> On arriving at Bunker Hill, General Putnam ordered part of [Gardner's regiment] to assist in throwing up defenses commenced at this place. One company went to the rail fence. The greater part, under the lead of their colonel, on the third advanced toward the redoubt. On the way, Colonel Gardner was struck by a ball, which inflicted a mortal wound. While a party was carrying him off, he had an affecting interview with his son, a youth of nineteen, who was anxious to aid in bearing him from the field. His heroic father prohibited him, and he was borne on a litter of rails over Winter Hill. Here he was overtaken

by retreating troops. He raised himself on his rude couch, and addressed to them cheering words. He lingered until July 3, when he died. On the fifth he was buried with the honors of war.[20]

Gardner died at the home of his sister, Elizabeth Sparhawk, on Western Avenue. General Washington, who had just arrived from Philadelphia to assume command of the revolutionary army, attended the services. Gardner was the second highest ranking American officer killed at Bunker Hill.[21] In 1785 the town of Gardner, Massachusetts was named in his memory.

Little Cambridge was touched in other ways by the American Revolution. The Roxbury Highway linking Boston to the towns north of the Charles River passed through Allston. Colonel Thomas Dawes, Paul Revere's associate in the midnight ride, used this road to alert the Minutemen of Concord that the British were coming. Later a British relief force under Lord Percy followed the same route. When Percy's force reached the Charles River, it was discovered that the local militia had removed the planks from the Great Bridge. Unfortunately, the pennywise colonials had neatly piled the planks on the opposite shore, which enabled the British to replace them with minimal delay. The militia then constructed a barricade at the southern end of the bridge, hoping to trap Percy on his return. The British commander frustrated this plan, however, by turning his force east at Harvard Square, thereby averting a confrontation that might have rivaled Lexington and Concord in importance.[22] During the eight month siege of Boston that followed, troops and mounted messengers passed up and down the Roxbury Highway between the headquarters of Generals Ward and Thomas in Roxbury and General Washington in Cambridge.[23]

The Roxbury Highway was not the only Little Cambridge road to witness events of the Revolution.

19

When Colonel Henry Knox transported the Fort Ticonderoga cannon to Dorchester Heights to force the British evacuation of Boston in March 1776, he moved them along the so-called Road to the Watertown Mill, the present Washington Street.[24]

While the great majority of her people warmly supported the revolution, as evidenced by the large number who served in the Continental Army, Little Cambridge had at least one resident loyalist—elderly Benjamin Faneuil. The Faneuil family's pro-British sentiments stemmed from several factors. According to a family history, they felt a strong attachment to Britain, a nation that had given their French Protestant family refuge from religious persecution in the 17th century. One suspects, however, that their extensive property interests in England and ties to British mercantile houses were of greater concern. Whatever losses they might suffer by virtue of their loyalist stance paled next to the high cost they would have been obliged to pay had they supported the revolution.

In 1760 Benjamin Faneuil, brother and heir to the public benefactor who gave Boston Faneuil Hall, retired to a 70-acre estate on the western end of Little Cambridge (west of the present Faneuil and Dunboy Street inter-section), turning the family business over to his sons. Benjamin Faneuil, Jr's decision to receive British tea during the crisis of 1773 made the family extremely unpopular. In 1774 the sons fled to England, leaving their aged father in the care of a sister, Mrs. Bethune. When the public learned of this flight, a mob marched on Faneuil Hall and destroyed a portrait of Peter Faneuil hanging there.

Benjamin Faneuil was over eighty years old in 1775. According to a family history he "had been blind for many years and never left his room except for an occasional drive in good weather." Perhaps fearing that her father's property would be seized by the revolutionary authorities, in the summer of 1775 Mrs. Bethune invited General Washington and some of his officers to dine at the Faneuil mansion. A family history furnishes the following account of that dinner:

When the day came the guests arrived; she had invited a few others to meet them, and all went charmingly. The dinner was over, the dessert on the table, when the door was flung wide and old Mr. Faneuil, leaning on the arm of his attendant, entered the apartment. All made room for him. He took his seat at the foot of the table, and told his guests he was very happy to find they had visited his house. Would they fill their glasses and allow him to drink their health? After a time when he had by listening found where Washington and Lee sat [General Arthur Lee, a deserter from the British Army] he turned toward Washington and said, "General Washington, I respect your character greatly; you act from patriotic motives, I have not a word to object to your course." But turning short on where Lee sat, "You General Lee, are fighting with a rope around your neck," etc. etc., expressing very plainly that he looked upon him as a traitor to king and country! The whole company rose from the table, and when they were taking leave General Washington said, "What does this mean, Mrs. Bethune?" "Can you not see what it means?" she asked; "My father has been blind and out of the world for twenty years, and he is now giving you the ideas in which he was educated."[25]

On her father's death in 1784, Mrs. Bethune inherited the Faneuil Estate. The family's connection with the property ended in 1811, when Mrs. Bethune's heirs sold the estate. The only surviving building, the Gatekeeper's House, dating from the 1760s, stands at the northwest

21

corner of Faneuil and Dunboy Streets, and is the oldest building in Oak Square.[26]

The most important event of the Revolutionary period was unquestionably the establishment of the Little Cambridge Cattle Market in 1775. The cattle industry quickly transformed Little Cambridge from a sleepy agricultural village into a thriving commercial center. The selling and butchering of cattle became the economic mainstay of the town for more than a century, profoundly influencing virtually every aspect of its economic, political, and social development.

The Cattle Market was established by two imaginative entrepreneurs, Jonathan Winship I and Jonathan Winship II, father and son. The Winships arrived in Little Cambridge from Lexington just before the Revolution.[27] From 1778 to 1780 Jonathan Winship II and his family lived in the Ebenezer Smith house, presently located at 17–19 Peaceable Street, the oldest structure in the Brighton Center area.[28]

Cambridge was the headquarters of the Continental Army from April 1775 to March 1776, and General Washington's troops needed provisioning. The Winships responded by putting out a call to the farmers of the outlying districts to send their cattle on the hoof to Little Cambridge. As the cattle arrived, they purchased and processed it for the army.[29] Their slaughterhouse stood near the present intersection of Chestnut Hill Avenue and Academy Hill Road.[30]

The original cattle yards were adjacent to the Bull's Head Tavern, which was located on Washington Street opposite the present Nantasket Avenue intersection.[31] The pens in which the incoming cattle were temporarily held probably stood on the flat land opposite the tavern, the area crossed today by Nantasket Avenue, Snow, and Shannon Streets. Since a stream ran through this property, it was particularly well suited for grazing.

22

The Winship family, founders of the Brighton Cattle Market, built this residence on the site of the present Brighton police station in 1780.

The importance of this contribution to the Patriot cause was noted by Willard M. Wallace in his military history of the American Revolution: "If a soldier's stomach is kept full, he can stand privation in other respects with a reasonable degree of cheerfulness. There were so few really hungry soldiers in the siege lines around Boston that winter that one might say it was with food rather than with troops and arms that Washington kept the British locked up in the city." [32]

By 1776, as the records of the Continental Army show, two Winship warehouses contained some 500 barrels of salted beef. So important was this supply, that the army posted soldiers to protect it against possible sabotage. [33]

23

The Winships quickly became the wealthiest family in Little Cambridge. In 1780 they built a large mansion on the site of the present Brighton Police Station.[34] By 1790 Jonathan Winship II (the elder Winship died in 1784) was the largest meatpacker in Massachusetts, putting up some 5,000 barrels of beef a year for foreign markets alone.[35]

The foundation of the Cattle Market was but the first of several singular contributions the Winship family made to the history of Allston-Brighton.

CHAPTER III

The Birth of Brighton

1790–1820

When the General Court authorized the incorporation of a separate parish in 1779, it gave Little Cambridge a significant measure of local self-determination. Eighteenth-century New England town life centered largely on its Congregational churches.

Little Cambridge waited until 1784 to settle a permanent minister, its choice falling ultimately to 21-year old John Foster, a recent graduate of Dartmouth College. Dr. Oliver Wendell Holmes later described this important figure, whose local career spanned more than forty years, as "mild-eyed John Foster, D.D. of Brighton with the lambent aurora of his smile about his pleasant mouth, which not even the sabbath could subdue to the true Levitical aspect."[1] Pietistic religion was on the wane in New England at the turn of the century, a decline nowhere more evident than in the commercial centers of eastern Massachusetts like Little Cambridge. Learned, kindly John Foster, author of more than thirty religious tracts, Harvard College Trustee, gentleman and aristocrat, was well-suited to the community he had been called to serve.[2]

Foster's wife Hannah is an even more interesting figure. Daughter of a wealthy Boston merchant, Grant Webster, Hannah was an accomplished writer. Her principal work, *The Coquette, or the History of Eliza Wharton*, was published in 1797. This shocking tale of seduction, based on the experiences of Rev. Foster's cousin, Elizabeth Whitman, became the most popular literary work in New England in

25

the early 1800s.[3] By 1840 it had appeared in some thirty editions. William Osborne, editor of the 1970 edition, noted that "Mrs. Foster [gave] early American fiction an interest it did not have before: a candid discussion of a social problem and a sensible depiction of character."[4]

John and Hannah Foster first lived in the old church parsonage on Academy Hill Road. They later built an elaborate house on Foster Street (then known as Dr. Foster's Lane), on the site of the Franciscan Sisters of Africa Convent, a location a contemporary described as "overlooking scenery as charming as any part of Brighton." Their residence was described as "a very large square house which faced to the south, to the front porch of which was added an ell used as a library and a reception room. The hilly land east of the house was terraced and the daughters became very industrious in keeping the grounds well stocked with flowering shurbs and plants."[5] Another source described the site as "just the place for a minister to write a sermon and romantic enough for his wife to write a novel."[6]

While the death of Colonel Thomas Gardner had robbed Little Cambridge of its strongest voice in town government, the community continued to exercise substantial influence in Cambridge town politics in the post-Revolutionary years. In each year from 1784 to 1793, Little Cambridge residents held two of Cambridge's seven Board of Selectmen seats, and in four out of ten of these years (1787–88 and 1792–93), Colonel Stephen Dana of Little Cambridge was the town's Representative to the General Court.[7] A farmer, carpenter, and butcher by occupation, Dana lived on a 50-acre estate on the south side of Oak Square. His gravestone in the old Market Street Burial Ground describes him as "a prudent, pleasant friend, the father, legislator, judge, and peacemaker of Brighton, extensively useful, and greatly beloved by all who knew him."[8]

26

Little Cambridge's influence in Cambridge government declined drastically, however, beginning in the mid-1790s. In contrast to the 1784 to 1793 period, when south-side residents held 26 percent of Cambridge's Board of Selectmen seats, representation in the 1794 to 1806 period fell to 15 percent. Moreover, after 1793 no Little Cambridge resident was elected Representative to the General Court.[9] The decline of influence stemmed from transportation and population changes brought about by the construction in 1793 of the West Boston Bridge over the Charles River linking the eastern end of Cambridge directly to Boston.

Prior to the construction of the West Boston Bridge, the only continuous route from Cambridge to Boston had been by way of the Great Bridge and the Roxbury Highway through Little Cambridge, Brookline, and Roxbury. A large portion of the travel to and from Boston, Cambridge historian Lucius Paige noted, "passed over the bridge in preference to the Charlestown Ferry."[10] After the construction of the West Boston Bridge, however, men and cattle used the much shorter West Boston Bridge route to the city, with two results for Little Cambridge: First, the upkeep of the Great Bridge was sadly neglected. Second, the population of the eastern end of Cambridge increased substantially. As Little Cambridge's share of the town's population diminished, so did its political influence.[11]

The people of Little Cambridge had resisted the change. In 1792, while the West Boston Bridge proposal was before the General Court, Little Cambridge joined Newton in voicing strong opposition on the grounds that the bridge would "create another obstruction to the navigation of the Charles River," would "greatly depreciate the property on said river," and that "no public advantages will be derived from the measure to compensate the private injuries that will be sustained."[12] Colonel Dana was Cambridge's Representative at the time. It was through him that the joint

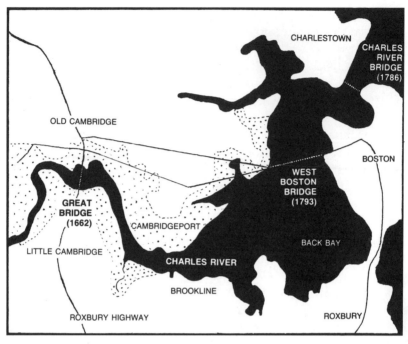

Map showing Charles River bridges as of 1800.

petition reached the floor of the House of Representatives. Cambridge proper and the communities to the north and west supported the project, while Little Cambridge, Newton, Brookline, and Roxbury vigorously objected.[13] By opposing powerful Cambridge interests, Dana destroyed his political standing in the town. It is no coincidence that 1793, the year of the opening of the West Boston Bridge, also marked the end of his career as a Cambridge office-holder. Dana's loss of status foreshadowed Little Cambridge's loss.

As Paige noted, "most of the thoroughfares through [Cambridge] which were opened during many years" after

1793 "were constructed for the benefit" of one or the other of the rival bridge corporations. When Andrew Craigie proposed a Canal Bridge project in 1806, the so-called "Battle of the Bridges" began, a struggle between competing bridge interests that "for several years kept the town in constant excitement and turmoil."[14] The rival corporations agreed on one point, however. Any bridge or road building proposal that threatened to divert traffic to Little Cambridge must be defeated. When the residents of Little Cambridge petitioned the town in 1806 for a road to be "laid out from near the store of Jonathan Winship through the land of Edward Sparhawk, S. W. Pomeroy and Thomas Gardner," the petition was referred to a committee "to procure a discontinuance of said road."[15] The proposed highway, the present Cambridge Street, would give farmers from the north better access to the Little Cambridge Cattle Market. Cambridge's refusal to authorize construction of this road was the catalyst for separation.

In February 1806 Benjamin Baker and sixty-six other residents of Little Cambridge presented the General Court with a petition asking "that all inhabitants of Cambridge on the south side of the Charles River may be incorporated as a distinct and separate town." While the petition cited distance from the seat of government as a major consideration, it was the portion dealing with the growing dissimilarity between the communities that revealed Little Cambridge's deepest concerns:

> To these considerations your petitioners conceive additional weight to be given by the changes that have taken place and are still to be expected in the relative state of the town, since the creation of the West Boston Bridge; the number of inhabitants in the other parishes has rapidly increased, and objects of enterprise have engrossed and are engrossing their

attention, alike irrelevant to the pursuits and advantage of your petitioners. Your petitioners therefore apprehend that the sameness which once proved a common bond and rendered it proper that they should make a part of the corporate body to which they have hitherto belonged, no more exists.[16]

The General Court referred the matter to the next session, but ordered that Little Cambridge's petition be published in two Boston papers for three successive weeks, "that all persons interested may then appear, and shew (sic) cause, if any they have, why the prayer of said petition should not be granted." Significantly, no opposition whatsoever materialized. Cambridge had apparently concluded that it was in its own interest to allow Little Cambridge, with its hostility to various bridge and road building schemes, to go its own way.

The only action taken by Cambridge town meeting on separation were two orders. On April 6, 1806 the town voted that "Caleb Gannett, Aaron Hill, and William Winthrop, Esqs and Deacon Josiah Moore and Mr. Daniel Mason be chosen a committee to confer with such persons as may be appointed by those who have petitioned the Legislature that the South Parish in this town be set off as a separate town."[17] The second order, dated July 6, 1806, directed "that the town choose a committee to attend the Legislature on the petition . . . to show what terms, conditions and limitations, the said town will consent to the incorporation of said parish and precinct into a separate town."[18]

When the General Court finally authorized the establishment of the independent Town of Brighton, the conditions and limitations it imposed were unremarkable. "Nothing in the act shall be construed," the legislation read, "to impair the right or privilege" of Brighton's Congretational minister at Harvard College. It also

30

required that Brighton pay its share of the Cambridge town debt, Middlesex County taxes, and the maintenance of the Great Bridge, as well as support of the Cambridge Poor House until such time as one of its own was established. With this act of February 24, 1807, Little Cambridge became the independent Town of Brighton.[19]

By the time the General Court passed the enabling act, the people of Little Cambridge had selected the name Brighton for the new corporate entity. According to historian J.P.C. Winship, the name was chosen at a public meeting. The records of that gathering are unfortunately lost. Winship theorized that the town was named after Brighton, England.[20] Another theory, advanced by literary historian Philip Van Doren Stern, is that it was named for a "bright," or prize ox, an allusion to the Brighton Cattle Market.[21]

While Brighton was winning its independence from Cambridge, Jonathan Winship II's sons were contributing significantly to the development of American commerce in the Pacific. Not content to follow his father into the meat-packing business, eldest son Abiel established a mercantile trading business with Benjamin Homer of Boston. By 1795, the firm of Homer and Winship owned a fleet of eight vessels.[22] Four of Jonathan's five sons entered this business, which specialized in trade with the Pacific. Abiel, who never went to sea, planned and financed the expeditions which his brothers commanded. The route the Winships followed—via Cape Horn, California, Alaska, Hawaii, and China—was some 22,000 miles long. A round trip often took three years to complete. The Pacific trade was dangerous, time-consuming, and costly, but offered enormous profit to men of courage and stamina.

Charles Winship, Jonathan's second son, was the first of the family to venture into the Pacific, sailing in 1797 as supercargo of the vessel *Alexander*. Upon his return, he was given command of the *Betsy*, a Homer & Winship

31

vessel, which became the first American ship to unfurl its flag in the California seal and otter hunting grounds. This venture ended in tragedy for the Winships, however, when Captain Charles, arrested and imprisoned by the Spanish on a charge of poaching, died from the effects of a "malignant fever of the climate."[23]

At this point, Joseph O'Cain, a former British naval officer, presented Jonathan and Abiel Winship with an intriguing business proposition. He proposed that they form a partnership for the purpose of opening up trade with Russian Alaska—that they transport supplies to Alaska to exchange for furs. He would also endeavor to persuade the Governor of Alaska, Alexander Baranov, with whom he was personally acquainted, to equip them with a force of Aleut hunters for otter and seal expeditions to the California coast. The proceeds of the expeditions would be divided between Baranov, the Winships, and O'Cain, with the Russian share going back to the Winships to pay for supplies. The Winships readily agreed to this proposal. They built a 280-ton vessel specifically for this trade, which they named in honor of their new business partner. A first class vessel of the day, complete with copper hull, the O'Cain set sail for the Pacific on January 3, 1803, with Jonathan Winship's fourth son, Jonathan III, serving as First Mate.

The Winships became the principal supplier of goods to Alaska—its life line to the outside world. Baranov readily agreed to the proposal for joint seal and otter hunting expeditions. These ventures proved highly lucrative. An 1807 expedition, for example, utilizing 150 Aleuts and 80 native canoes, yielded a profit of $136,000, an immense sum for the day. The Winships' successes in this trade soon earned them the title "Lords of the Pacific."[24]

The collaboration with Baranov also had its disappointing aspects. The Winships had hoped to win an outright monopoly of the transportation of Alaskan furs to China.

32

By 1808, however, the ships of several other nations were offering the Americans serious competition. Baranov would have no part of the monopoly scheme. He was building his own fleet with a view to eliminating all foreign involvement in the Alaskan trade.[25]

In an effort to strengthen their competitive position, the Winships decided to establish a trading post on the Columbia River mid-way between Alaska and the California hunting ground. They hoped not only to open up a profitable trade in furs with the local Indians, but also to produce crops to be used in trade with Alaska.

The command of the Columbia River expedition was given to Jonathan's third son, Nathan. The vessel *Albatross* was sent out from Boston with every article necessary for the establishment of a permanent settlement. In his letter of instruction, Abiel directed his brother

> to select a site thirty miles up the river and purchase the land from the natives; build a large two-story house, in the second story of which all the common muskets and ammunition should be placed with portholes in the side, and holes for musketry in the floor. The entrance to the second floor should be a single trap door, the ladder to be hauled up after the people ascend; and in no wise should a native be allowed on that floor. It is also enjoined to clear up and to cultivate a piece of land, under the protection of the guns and never have less than half of the men on guard; the object of the trade [being] to procure the skins of sea otter, mink, fox, bear, sable, muskrat, and, in fact, any production suitable for the China or American market.

The *Albatross* arrived on the Columbia in late May 1819. Captain Nathan chose a site on the south bank about thirty miles up the river. On June 4 the crew began construction of a fort. Four days later they were flooded out and moved to another site a quarter of a mile downstream. Just as work started again, a massing of Chinook Indians forced the abandonment of the project.[26] Though unsuccessful, this was the first attempt to establish an American post in the Pacific Northwest. As historians Dorothy Johansen and Charles Gates noted in their history of the Columbia River Valley, the Winships were in the forefront of those "enterprising mercantile interests [that] saw the Columbia River as a vital link in an enlarged commerce involving Russian Alaska, Spanish California, the Hawaiian Islands, the Orient, and parts of southern Europe and South America. The Winships were pioneers of the idea "that the Columbia River should become the western depot of a trade that spanned a continent."[27]

The Winships' next theater of operations was the Hawaiian sandalwood trade. A fragrant wood, greatly in demand in the Orient, sandalwood was used in making idols for Buddhist temples, as well as carved boxes, incense sticks, and also as a fuel in funeral rites. The Winships began the active commercial exploitation of sandalwood.[28]

In March 1810 they rendered a signal service to the Emperor of Hawaii, Kamehameha I, by persuading the King of Kauai to place himself under the Emperor's protection, thus completing the unification of the Hawaiian Islands. The Winships transported the ruler of Kauai, Kauma-lii, to the court of Kamehameha in Honolulu. Richard Tregaskis, biographer of Kamehameha, describing Kauma-lii's arrival in Honolulu, noted:

> With this regal party stood Captain Nathan Winship, skipper of the O'Cain, trader *par excellence* and now the amateur diplomat who had brought the two feuding chiefs together.

34

Like the other traders with a humanitarian streak, the Winships were more interested in trade for articles of peace, like sandalwood, than selling guns to warring chiefs. They had the vision to see that a united and prosperous kingdom of Hawaii would be a much fatter treasure for them than a feuding island archipelago constantly devastated by war.[29]

History also credits the Winships with introducing bricks and horses to the Hawaiian Islands. The term for brick in Hawaiian, *pohaku winihepa*, means "Winship stones."[30] In July 1812 Kamehameha granted the Winships a monopoly over the Hawaiian sandalwood trade. They had little opportunity to exploit the economic privilege, however. The outbreak of war with Great Britain in 1812 prevented them from doing so. Finding the Winships unable to meet the terms of their agreement, Kamehameha gave way to mounting British pressure and cancelled the monopoly.[31]

The most significant direct influence of these adventures on the history of Brighton may well have been the knowledge Jonathan Winship III gained of horticulture while living in China. Jonathan spent his last two years in the Pacific as a resident of the foreign compound in Whampoa.[32] A contemporary described life in Whampoa as "cabined, cribbed, confined to an impossible degree." One privilege the authorities allowed foreigners, however, was the opportunity to visit the Fati Gardens on the opposite shore of the Pearl River. It was there that Jonathan Winship, who founded the horticultural industry in Brighton, learned the rudiments of the science he was later to practice so successfully in his native town.[33]

CHAPTER IV

The Flowering of Brighton
1820–1850

Brighton's first town meeting in March 1807 created thirty-four public offices. Since there were only two hundred qualified voters (the town's population was less than 500), there was ample opportunity for public office-holding. As Alexis de Toqueville later wrote, town meeting government was "to liberty what primary schools are to science; they bring it within the people's reach, they teach men how to use and enjoy it."

After electing Colonel Stephen Dana Town Clerk, the meeting named Nathaniel Champney, Thomas Gardner, Jr., Jonathan Livermore, Dudley Hardy, and Benjamin Hill as Brighton's first Board of Selectmen. Colonel Dana was also elected Representative to the Massachusetts General Court. There was a good deal of multiple office-holding: Thomas Gardner, Jr., for example, simultaneously held the posts of Selectman, Fence Viewer, Surveyor of Highways, and Town Ward.[1]

Brighton had one church in 1807, and it was entitled under law to public support. After increasing the Rev. Foster's salary, a subscription was initiated to replace the 1744 church edifice which the community had outgrown. Some sixty families subscribed to this fund; ultimately each was obliged to contribute $170.[2] The town moved the 1744 church across Washington Street to the site of the present Elk's Lodge. The first floor was converted into two

36

school rooms and the second used as a Town Hall until 1841.

Ebenezer Parsons, a prominent citizen, donated the bell for the new church. On the day it was to be raised to the belfry, he went to the nearby schoolhouse and requested that the students come to the church and take hold of the rope so "that they might ever after remember the fact by being able to say they had assisted at the raising."[3]

While the townspeople willingly supported their minister and paid for a modern church structure befitting a prosperous commercial center, religion was apparently not a matter of deep concern. Rev. Foster's dedication sermon suggests something less than uniform piety in Brighton for it chastised those who "have no just conception of the sacredness either of the time or place . . . who engage without reluctance in the discussion of secular topics, and often communicate intelligence and make arrangements of a business nature at the very threshold of the sanctuary," and who sometimes, "not content with the frivolous conversation and behavior abroad . . . carry the same spirit within the consecrated walls."[4]

A more forceful figure than Foster might have prevented the schism in his congregation that occurred just six months before retirement in 1827—the withdrawal of a dissatisfied conservative minority and the establishment, under the Rev. George Blagden, of the Brighton Evangelical Congregational Society.

According to a history of the Congregational Church,

the state of religion in Brighton before the introduction of orthodox preaching was alarmingly low.
The old Minister, Dr. Foster, was a Unitarian; his
preaching produced little effect. Being situated in
high life, his visits were complained of as being
partial; he became unpopular, his meetings were little
attended and his influence small. The dissatisfaction

37

with Dr. Foster and the division in his parish led to the introduction of evangelical preaching. The enemies of Dr. Foster were willing to support any preaching that would pull him down.[5]

This 1827 breach in the First Church was hardly unique. Similar schisms occurred in hundreds of New England churches in this period. While more orthodox preaching might have held the conservatives, it might also have driven the congregation's Universalists and Deists into open revolt. It would, in any event, have violated Dr. Foster's basic nature. "I cannot think," wrote George Livermore, historian of the First Church, "that a belief either in an angry God, a burning hell, or a lost soul could have found a place in his gentle heart."[6]

Brighton was now in a position to build a system of roads to better serve the community's burgeoning cattle industry. Construction of the present Cambridge Street was immediately begun. Though the project entailed considerable expense (substantial movement of earth being required to create a passable roadbed), the project was carried forward rapidly.[7] Cambridge Street provided only a partial solution to the northern access problem. A bridge across the Charles River was also required.

On March 2, 1808 Samuel Wyllys Pomeroy, a major Brighton landowner and cattle dealer, Jonathan Loring Austin of Cambridge, and four other "real estate owners" formed the Brighton and Cambridgeport Bridge Corporation for the purpose of constructing a bridge linking Cambridge Street to Cambridgeport and points north. Brighton welcomed the proposal, offering to support half the cost of the toll bridge's maintenance "after it is well built." This bridge, the fourth on the Charles River, opened to traffic on December 11, 1810. Road and bridge building and maintenance were matters of major concern to the Town of Brighton throughout the first half of the 19th century.[8]

38

In 1813 Brighton acquired a distinguished new resident, the Reverend Dr. Noah Worcester, editor of the Unitarian journal *The Christian Disciple* and one of the founders of the American peace movement. Worcester wrote his most important work, *A Solemn Review of the Custom of War* (1814), in Brighton. It was widely circulated in the United States and abroad and led to the establishment of many peace societies, including the Massachusetts Peace Society which Worcester served as Secretary. From 1818 to 1828 Worcester edited the Pacifist journal *The Friend of Peace*.[9]

Dr. Worcester lived at the northwest corner of Washington and Foster Street at the western end of Brighton Center. He was Brighton's first postmaster, serving from 1817 until his death in 1837.[10] It is not clear why it took the Postal Department ten years to establish a post office in Brighton, or how local mail was handled prior to 1817.

On his return from the Pacific in 1816, Jonathan Winship III moved into the Winship mansion. According to his son, the historian J.P.C. Winship, he laid out a hot bed of flowers opposite the house. In the following year he increased the number and variety of blooms and began offering them for sale. Then, in 1821, taking his youngest brother Francis as a partner, he moved the enterprise to a 37-acre property in North Brighton, a tract that extended from the intersection of Faneuil and Market Streets to the banks of the Charles River. The present aptly-named Vineland Street runs through the heart of this acreage.[11]

Jonathan Winship soon became one of New England's leading horticulturists. In 1829 he helped establish the Massachusetts Horticultural Society, serving as First Vice President from 1835 to 1847, the year of his death.[12] J.P.C. Winship described Winship Gardens as follows:

There were three avenues through Winship Gardens from North Beacon Street to the depot [The Boston & Worcester built a depot in the Gardens in 1834]—

one directly behind the old residence shaded by trees, the second along Market Street between borders of plants, and the third by a field of rose bushes. The latter led to a bridge over the railroad which with another at the westerly part of the nursery connected the grounds.

On the grounds were several arbors where visitors and passengers by the railroad could rest. One of them was an expensive affair. It was called the Moss House and was adorned with many articles from China, including birds, animals, and reptiles. It was burned by sparks from an engine. Between Market Street and the first bridge alluded to, the grounds were terraced and very carefully adorned with flowering plants and shrubs.

May Day was distinguished by the elite of Boston riding horseback early in the morning to Winship's Gardens, there purchasing a bouquet, and thence returning, by way of Roxbury, to attend May Day exercises or to return to their homes for Breakfast. It was a fad that continued in fashion for many years. The Winships would sell three to five hundred bouquets on that day and were dependent for additional flowers upon many other producers in the country about the city.

The Conservatory in Winship's Gardens was a feature. It was about one hundred feet long and fifty feet wide. Its main passageway was tiled with marble and bordered with blue Chinaware about two feet high. The front lower walk was similarly treated. The rear of the building was used for potting plants and arranging flowers, with a room for preparing seeds and storing buds.

The Winship family sold the property following Francis Winship's death in the late 1840s. In 1856 the tract was subdivided into house lots which were sold at public auction.[13]

In 1820 Joseph L.L.F. Warren established Brighton's second horticultural firm. His nursery, Nonantum Vale Gardens, situated at the southwest corner of Lake and Washington Streets, west of Brighton Center, attracted such eminent visitors as Ralph Waldo Emerson, Daniel Webster, John C. Calhoun, Henry Wadsworth Long-fellow, and William Cullen Bryant. Warren and Bryant were intimate friends for over forty years, according to Winship. Warren won many prizes including an 1838 award from the Boston Horticultural Society for raising the first tomatoes in Massachusetts.[14]

The third major horticultural business established in Brighton was that of Joseph Breck, dating from 1836. The author of an outstanding horticultural treatise, *The Young Florist, or Conversations on the Culture of Flowers and on Natural History*, Breck came to Brighton from Lancaster, Massachusetts, having served as Superintendent of the Horticultural Gardens there. As editor of the *New England Farmer*, he was already a leading figure. The prior success of the Winships and Warren is probably what attracted him to Brighton.

Breck's first Brighton nursery was located at the corner of Washington and Allston Streets, near the Brookline line. At first he specialized in raising vegetables and flower seeds, but afterwards added shrubs, bulbous rooted plants, phlox, peonies, and tulips. In 1851 he discontinued this nursery, selling most of its stock to his son-in-law William C. Strong for use at the grapery he had recently acquired from Horace Gray on Nonantum Hill.

Breck resumed his career as a Brighton nurseryman in 1854 at a new location, the northwest corner of Nonantum and Washington Streets in Oak Square, laying

THE ANCIENT OAK, AT BRIGHTON, MASS.

The Great White Oak, the largest such tree in Massachusetts, and the first Oak Square School stood on the green at Oak Square. The engraving dates from the early 1850s.

out the gardens behind his residence on the parcel of land now occupied by the Oak Square School. Breck served as President of the Massachusetts Horticultural Society from 1859 to 1862.[15]

Another important horticultural establishment was founded by Horace Gray on Nonantum Hill in the early 1840s. According to Wilder's *The Horticulture of Boston and*

42

Vicinity, he "erected on the grounds the largest grape-houses known in the United States, in which were grown extensively numerous varieties of foreign grapes. For the testing of these under glass in cold houses, Gray erected a large curvilinear-roof house, two-hundred feet long by twenty-four wide. This was such a great success that he built two more of the same dimension."[16]

The Brighton grapery was but one of Gray's many enter-prises. His attorney, Daniel Webster, frequently sent a young law clerk, William S. Strong, to Gray's Nonantum Hill estate on business. According to Winship, Strong "was so charmed with the estate and especially the graperies that in the following year, 1848, when the estate was sold at auction he became the purchaser. The size of the estate, over one hundred acres, and the magnitude of the graperies . . . became at once such an interest and such a burden that he gave up the profession of law and devoted himself to horticultural interests."[17]

Strong expanded on Gray's operation by laying out additional vines and adding other plants to the nursery's output. He also built an immense greenhouse, in which, Wilder noted, "under one continuous roof of glass of 18,000 square feet, is an enclosure where plants are grown in the open ground; where immense quantities of the rose and flowers are daily cut for the market."[18]

In 1855 Strong excavated Chandler's Pond at the southern edge of his property, leasing the pond and adjacent ice houses to Malcolm Chandler, an ice dealer, who later purchased the property. In 1865 Strong exca-vated a second pond west of Chandler's, on the Newton boundary. This body of water, Strong's Pond, has since been filled in.[19]

Though not as prominent, other Brighton residents contributed significantly to the practice of horticulture in the 19th century. Gorham Parsons, a founder of the Massachusetts Horticultural Society, experimented in fruit cultivation at his Brighton estate, Oakland Farms. Samuel Wyllys Pomeroy ran his estate on the most advanced agricultural principles of the day, as did Samuel Brooks, who employed Thomas Needham, former gardener to Horace Gray.[20] The "North End" farms of Abel Rice and the Scott brothers on Everett Street were the principal suppliers of strawberries to the Boston market after 1840. The Scott brothers introduced several new varieties of the fruit: the Scott Seedling, Lady of the Lake, and the Brighton Pine, among others.[21] By 1850 Brighton was one of the leading horticultural centers in New England.

The town's importance as an agricultural center was enhanced by the 1818 decision of the Massachusetts Society for Promoting Agriculture to locate its fair grounds and exhibition hall permanently in Brighton. One of the earliest and largest agricultural fairs in the nation, the Brighton Fair and Cattle Show, was held in October of each year from 1817 to 1835. Recognizing that a permanent location of the fair in Brighton would greatly benefit the local cattle industry, the town fathers were more than happy to accede to the MSPA's request for "permanent regulations to secure order" and an "accommodation of land."[22]

Brighton's eagerness to obtain the cattle show is evidenced by the care it took in selecting a site. Samuel Wyllys Pomeroy, owner of the Bull's Head Tavern, anxious to have the exhibition hall located adjacent to his hostelry, offered the MSPA one half acre on either side of its hall, as well as the use of ten acres on the opposite side of the highway as long as the cattle show was held in Brighton. The town rejected this offer, however, noting that "as every eye has been directed to a field owned by Mr. A[biel] Winship fronting the public house as being the most eligible situation," they would do their best to secure that property.[23]

The land in question was situated where the Winship

44

School now stands at the top of Dighton Street. The largest public house in Brighton, Hastings Tavern, stood nearby on Washington Street. The town had little difficulty persuading Abiel Winship to deed this land to the MSPA.[24]

The science of agriculture made significant advances in Massachusetts in the early 1800s through the efforts of the MSPA. Though the Society's offices were located in Boston, according to its own history, its most important activity was its annual Cattle Show and Fair. These fairs, held in Brighton until 1835, "embraced everything that could interest a farmer or be of benefit to agriculture; and in connection with them the importation of superior breeds of farm animals laid a firm and scientific base for the excellence which developed later."[25]

The Fair was held in October. Weeks before it was due to open, display items began arriving at the Society's exhibition hall on Agricultural Hill, as the Brighton location came to be known. The two-story structure, standing on "beautiful and elevated grounds," was seventy by thirty-six feet long. The lower level was used to display the latest farm implements and mammoth vegetables, while the upper level was devoted to textile and handicraft exhibits. Cattle pens were laid out on the slopes of the hill.[26]

The fair began with a procession from the exhibition hall to the First Church where the minister invoked God's blessings on the occasion. The awards were then announced by the various committees. In 1829 prizes were awarded in the following categories: fat cattle, bulls and bull calves, cows and heifers, sheep and swine, inventions, butter and cheese, cider, grain and vegetables, ploughing, and manufacturing. A 17-pound turnip, a 19-pound radish, and a bough on which pears hung like a cluster of grapes were among the outstanding exhibits of that year. After the distribution of the awards a sumptuous meal was served and speeches heard on agricultural topics.[27]

By 1830 the Brighton Fair was in decline owing to "the effects of counter attractions by the county societies." The last fair was held in 1835. The speakers on that occasion included Daniel Webster, Edward Everett, Abbott Lawrence, and Supreme Court Justice Joseph Story. In 1844 the MSPA sold the fair grounds for $6,000.[28] The exhibition hall was moved off the hill to the southeast corner of Washington Street and Chestnut Hill Avenue, becoming the Eastern Market Hotel. This structure, the oldest in Brighton Center, is still standing. The acreage was subdivided and sold at public auction.[29]

Control of the fishing grounds on the Charles River, long a source of contention between the towns of Cambridge and Watertown and now a troublesome issue in the relationship between Brighton and Watertown, was finally resolved by an act of the legislature in 1827, placing control of the grounds in the hands of a board of five fish wardens (three from Watertown and two from Brighton), who were authorized to take fish "at such times, in such manner, with such seines, nets, utensils, and machinery, and by such persons, agents, or servants as they may see fit to employ," the profits from the enterprise to be divided between Watertown and Brighton on a 70–30 percent basis.[30]

In 1825 two major new roads were added to Brighton's developing transportation system. A causeway called the Mill Dam Road had been built across the Back Bay to present Kenmore Square in 1820. An extension of this highway was now constructed through Brighton following the line of Commonwealth Avenue, Brighton Avenue, and North Beacon Street to the North Beacon Street Bridge (built in 1822). The Mill Dam project had the enthusiastic backing of Brighton's leaders, some of whom owned stock in the enterprise.

The second new road was Western Avenue, a project of the Proprietors of the West Boston Bridge. Since this road would carry traffic around rather than through the commercial heart of the community, it was strongly opposed by the people of Brighton. Despite a strongly worded protest from the town, a bill authorizing the project passed the Legislature and the objectionable highway was constructed.[31]

By the late 1820s, the rivalry between the West Boston Bridge and Mill Dam Road corporations was assuming a new focus—the route to be followed by a projected Boston to Worcester railroad. If this railroad were built in a direct line across Back Bay into Brighton, it would prove a boon to the town's flourishing cattle market. If, instead, it crossed the Charles River into East Cambridge or Cambridgeport, Brighton's primacy would be seriously threatened.

The route ultimately chosen for the Boston & Worcester Railroad crossed the Back Bay into the northern and least populated section of Brighton. The Massachusetts Board of Internal Improvements described the area as follows:

> The road in Brighton will be level for nearly three miles, and five feet above the level of the marsh. Bridges of wood will be necessary across the channels of the river and across the flats an earth embankment, supported by side walls of stone, and across the marshes, by a foundation on piles and an embankment. Thence to the river again opposite the Arsenal, and along its right bank and the side hill to Mr. Hunnewell's in Newton.[32]

According to Winship, Gorham Parsons, a major Brighton landowner and State Representative in 1820 and 1821, was instrumental in the selection of this route rather than a more southerly one that would have taken the railroad through the center of the town.[33] Construction of the Boston & Worcester Railroad began in 1832.

47

The coming of the railroad to Brighton on April 4, 1834 was an occasion of great joy to the people of Brighton, who lined the tracks around the Brighton Depot in Winship Gardens to welcome the first B&W locomotive, a single car containing the officers of the company who were making a trial run to the end of the line, then finished to West Newton.[34] The building of the B&W through Brighton marked the culmination of the town's long struggle to solidify its hold on the cattle trade. Since the railroad encouraged livestock shipments to Brighton by setting low carload rates for cattle, sheep, hogs, and calves, its construction proved highly beneficial to the town's economy.[35]

The construction of the railroad through Brighton proved equally beneficial to the Boston & Worcester Corporation. In the early years, receipts at the Brighton Station exceeded those of any other depot on the line, including the Boston and Worcester depots.[36]

The importance of the railroad is clear from the following description of Brighton, written a dozen years after the construction of the Boston & Worcester:

Brighton is the first regular station on the road. The village is about a half mile south of the railroad, and is famous as being the largest cattle market in New England. Large numbers of cattle, sheep and swine are brought daily over the railroad from the western part of the state, to be disposed of here. The Brighton station is directly within Winship's Gardens, a lovely spot indeed. It is open at all times to the public, and to those who are travelling for pleasure, it is well worth a visit. Fruit trees, shrubbery, plants and flowers of every description, cover the whole enclosure, which is nearly twenty-five acres in extent. Like Brookline, and other towns near Boston, Brighton has become the residence of many people of wealth, who have erected costly residences.

48

All was not positive in this 1846 description, however. It also called attention to "the extensive and numerous butchering establishments, which are scattered over the town," constituting "a serious objection to the choice of Brighton as a place of residence, unconnected with the business."[37] This public health issue would grow more and more critical with the years.

CHAPTER V

Brighton in the 1850s

Adam's *Almanac for 1850* described Brighton as "more varied and beautiful . . . than any town around Boston." It was served by an excellent system of roads and bridges and "omnibuses and cars . . . connect it with the city by frequent and easy communication."[1] The new Greek Revival town hall, designed and built in 1841 by local architect Granville Fuller, symbolized the community's flourishing condition.

Brighton, in fact, attained its high water mark as a commercial center in the 1850s. The Cattle Market, New England's largest, was doing some $2 to 3 million of business in hogs, cattle, and sheep annually.[2] The town contained, in addition, some fifty small-scale butchering establishments. One in seven Brighton families earned its livelihood from butchering. When one adds to this the many drovers, stockmen, and cattle dealers residing in the town, the cattle industry's pervasive influence becomes clear.

The novelist Nathaniel Hawthorne wrote the following description of the Brighton Cattle Market in the fall of 1840:

Thursday of every week, which by common consent and custom is the market day, changes the generally quiet village of Brighton into a scene of bustle and excitement. At early morning the cattle, sheep etc. are hurried in and soon the morning train from Boston, omnibuses, carriages and other "vehicular mediums" bring a throng of drovers, buyers, speculators and spectators; so that, by 10 o'clock, there are generally gathered as many as two or three hundred vehicles in the area fronting the Cattle Fair Hotel. The proprietors thereof throng the spacious barroom for the purpose of warming themselves in winter, and in summer "cooling off"—the process for effecting both results being precisely the same.

The portico of the hotel is occupied by hawkers and peddlers, who sell clothing, jewelry, soap, watches, knives, razors, etc. (to say nothing of their customers), at astonishingly low rates. An "English hunting lever eighteen carots fine," is frequently sold for five or six dollars, and, of course, is a genuine article. In the region round about, "Mammoth Steer," "Living Skeletons," "Snakes," etc., are on exhibition at reasonable prices.

One of the outside features of the market is the horse auction. A Brighton horse has become a proverb. Here are gathered all the old, wornout, broken-down, and used-up omnibus, cart and livery stable steeds, and these are knocked down (if they don't tumble down) at sums varying from five to forty dollars. These sales are productive of a great deal of merriment and the mettle, speed and fine points of the animals are exhibited (the "points" perhaps being sufficiently prominent already).

All this time the butchers and the drovers are busily engaged in their traffic. The fattest and best of the cattle in their pens find ready sale, and long before all the drovers are in, select lots begin to be driven from the grounds. Men and boys hurry up and down the

51

Cattle Fair Hotel and cattle yards on Market Day (1856).

53

lanes and through the pens, each armed with a stick which is a sort of shillelah, shouting to the half-crazed cattle, and with screams and blows directing them where they should go. Occasionally a drove of cows and calves come along, the latter muzzled, and the former looing and bellowing in chorus to the shouts of their drivers. Farmers from the neighboring towns are selecting "stores" from the large number of that class in the pens, and dairymen carefully examining the "milky mothers" that are so anxiously seeking their young from the midst of their companions. Working oxen are driven in by farmers from the vicinity, who sell, only after much banter, to buy again when prices are low. In the midst of these, dogs, and goats and mules are offered for sale, and nearby, are the hog pens, containing at this season, only stores, which are sold singly and in pairs to small farmers, mechanics and others who think they can afford to "keep a pig."

The forenoon is busy enough. At high noon the huge bell of the hotel announces dinner, and for a brief period there is a breathing spell for man and beast. After dinner, business again resumes its sway. The voice of the hawker becomes hoarse, but it is by no means silenced. Drovers who have not made many sales get nervous, and the pens are cleared out without much regard to profit on the part of the seller. The butchers begin to turn their faces home-wards and the drovers, generally with well-filled wallets, start for Boston. A few, not liking the prices, and hoping for "better times," make arrangements to turn out their cattle to pasture, and hold over to another week. By five o'clock the business of the day is over, and Brighton subsides once more into a quiet, matter-of-fact Massachusetts village, till another Thursday brings round another market day.[3]

54

Cattle Market customers needed overnight accommodations which were provided by several hotels. The largest, as Hawthorne noted, was the Cattle Fair at the northwest corner of Washington and Market Streets on Market Square. Built in 1830, on a design of Zachariah B. Porter, it was advertised as "having been arranged with particular attention to the traveller and drover, both as to comfort and convenience."[4] In 1852 it was enlarged in the then popular Italianate style by the noted Boston architect William Washburn. Additions included a third story, portico of rusticated stone, cupola, bracketed cornices and ballustrades, and broad verandas from which the guests could admire the vistas and cattle dealers take shelter from the sun and rain. Its one hundred rooms made it the largest hotel in suburban Boston. A dance hall ran the entire length of the top floor. As many as four to five hundred guests are said to have dined at one time in its spacious banquet hall. To the rear stood the cattle pens and auction platform of the Brighton Cattle Market.[5]

Another important hotel of the period was the Brighton Hotel, the converted Winship mansion, which stood on the site of the present Police Station. Samuel Dudley purchased the mansion from the Winships in 1820, adding a second story to the structure.[6] General LaFayette stayed at the Brighton Hotel in June 1825 when he visited the town during his second American tour.

Other hotels included the Eastern Market Hotel at the southwest corner of Washington Street and Chestnut Hill Avenue, and Goding's Hotel on Western Avenue (the old Sparhawk mansion).[7]

The commercial vitality of Brighton led to the establishment of the Newton Street Railway in 1858. The cars of this horse railway company ran from Newton to Boston by way of Washington and Cambridge Streets, Cambridge and the West Boston Bridge.[8]

Brighton's commercial vitality also led to the establishment of banks at an early date. These institutions had colorful and controversial histories. The Bank of Brighton, established in 1828, went out of business in 1830 when a run left it holding liabilities totalling more then $265,000. It was succeeded in March 1832 by a second Bank of Brighton with leading citizen Gorham Parsons as President. Capitalized at $150,000, this institution functioned fairly responsibly for some years. In 1858, however, Thomas Hunt, a North Brighton Merchant, filed a petition with the state legislature charging the bank with "unlawful practices and transactions." A legislative committee investigated and found numerous irregularities that "reflected great discredit upon the bank." Despite these charges, the Bank of Brighton continued in operation until 1883.[9]

In 1854 the Brighton Market Bank was established. Floated with $100,000 of capital in the boom preceding the Panic of 1857, at a time when there were no effective controls, it was managed with great efficiency by its President, Life Baldwin. During some seventy years of existence, it never experienced a run and always declared an annual dividend, even in the depths of a national depression.[10] It survived until 1923 when it was absorbed by the First National Bank of Boston. In the 1850s the Bank of Brighton and the Brighton Market Bank stood on Washington Street opposite the Cattle Fair Hotel.[11]

In addition to the cattle and horticultural industries, Brighton contained many small manufacturing establishments producing a wide range of products—buttons, soap, candles, tinware, shoes, boots, carriages, fireworks, harnesses, lard oil, pumps, sashes and blinds, whips, wheels, and varnish. Much of this manufacturing, it should be noted, was related to the cattle industry: soap, candles, shoes, boots, harnesses, blinds, whips, and varnish were all manufactured from livestock by-products. The local market gardening and horticultural industries, moreover, utilized the manure, offal, and bone fertilizer derived from the stockyard and slaughtering establishments of the town to enrich their acreage. A major part of this industry was concentrated on or near Western Avenue adjacent to the Charles River mudflats, an area unsuited for residential development.[12] The Charles River was an important commercial artery at mid-century. Vessels of several hundred tons navigated the river as far as Brighton where wharves for lumber, coal, and lime were situated.[13]

As a wealthy commercial town, Brighton could afford civic amenities. It had outgrown the half-acre Market Street Burial Ground years earlier. By the 1850s wealthy communities were building new rural or garden-type cemeteries. The outstanding example was Mt. Auburn in Cambridge. By contrast with the simple church burial grounds of earlier days, these rural cemeteries were laid out by landscape architects for beauty and picturesqueness. Visitors often picnicked among the monuments and gravestones.

Brighton's Evergreen Cemetery was a smaller version of Mt. Auburn. Aspinwall Woods, a fourteen-acre tract on South Street (now Commonwealth Avenue) in the remote southwest corner of town, was chosen as the site. The natural contours of the land were preserved. Avenues and paths were laid out with an eye to picturesque effect. The plan even called for the construction of a chapel at the center of the cemetery; instead, a Civil War monument occupies the site. The Reverend Frederick Augustus Whitney, Minister of the First Church, gave the 1850 dedicatory sermon: "Be these whispering groves, be the storied monuments and engraven stones, as they shall presently stand here in solemn silence, impressive preachers to us all! Here, in peace, may we commune with the spirit land."[14]

Brighton's public schools saw steady improvement in the

1840s and 1850s. The first Brighton School Committee was elected in 1820.[15] Until 1840, however, there were only four schoolhouses in the town—the central school, dating from 1722, in Brighton Center; the Oak Square School, established in 1825, on the green under the historic White Oak; the eastern school, established in 1832, on Cambridge Street near its intersection with Gordon Street; and the northern school, established in 1834, which stood on the site of the present Storrow School in North Brighton.[16] The town provided only the most basic schooling in these years; private academies existed for those desiring college preparation.

Relatively little is known about the local public schools prior to 1840, when the first annual school committee report was filed with Massachusetts Secretary of Education Horace Mann. Prior to the 1840s Brighton was best know for its excellent private institutions. These included a school established in 1800 by James Dana in the old Dana mansion on Washington Street near the Brookline line, a classical school for boys that Jacob Knapp established in 1805 at his residence on Bowen (Washington) Hill, as well as a school run by Hosea Hildreth that offered instruction in singing and music.[17] By the 1840s, however, Brighton was committing substantial sums to the improvement of public education. In two years in the early forties the town maintained the highest per capital expenditure for education in Massachusetts. By the early 1850s the Brighton Public Schools operated a high school, two grammar schools, and six elementary schools serving 600 students, a number exceeding the town's population at the time of the separation from Cambridge in 1807.[18]

The Brighton High School, established in 1841, was situated on upper Academy Hill Road in a building that had once served as a private academy. The high school sent it first graduates to college in 1850—William Wirt Warren to Harvard and Henry Baldwin to Yale. Both

58

passed the entrance exams with distinction. In 1855 the townspeople narrowly rejected a proposal to move the high school to Washington Street because the "almost constant passing and repassing, particularly on market days of horses, cattle, sheep, swine and vehicles of almost every description would endanger the health, lives and limbs of the pupils who should there congregate."[19] Finally, a larger structure was built on adjacent land in 1856 and the old building moved to the corner of Winship and Washington Streets.[20]

The high school students of the mid-19th century were apparently no better behaved than those of our day, though possibly somewhat more imaginative. According to Winship

> They first discovered that on very cold days by opening the upper furnace door the fire would so lessen in strength as to heat only one room, and the girls were necessarily invited to visit the lower room to see the boys.
>
> They further discovered that by putting cayenne pepper in the furnace the fumes would drive all the scholars and teachers out of the building—this they practiced. They muffled the bell in the belfry and were unable to know when to go to school, and many were very late.
>
> Up to that time the [sexes] were separate. By an initiative act of a few of the girls a wider aperture was made in the hall partition than any shrinking of boards would occasion. The partition dividing the school was removed, the School Committee deciding that coeducation was desirable.[21]

Brighton's two grammar schools, equivalent to today's middle or junior high schools, were located in Brighton

Town Hall and on North Harvard Street, near Western Avenue. When fire destroyed the North Harvard Street structure in 1853, a new school was built at a cost of $8,000.[22] The 1855 school committee report described this building as one that "would do honor to any town. Few in the state are superior to it."[23]

There were six primary schools in Brighton in the 1850s —District School #1 was located in the North Harvard Street Grammar School; District School #2 on the Storrow School site in North Brighton; District School #3 on the Oak Square green (when the Great White Oak was removed in 1855 a new schoolhouse was constructed to replace the 1825 structure); District School #4 in the High School on Academy Hill Road; District School #5 at Shepard and Washington Streets; and District School #6 at the corner of Brighton Avenue and Allston Street in Union Square.[24]

Brighton's concern for public education was not limited to the young. Throughout the 1850s distinguished speakers came to Brighton as part of the Lyceum Movement. Their lectures, paid for by the town, were held in the evenings in Town Hall and were open to all residents, young and old. Some of the more notable speakers included Charles Sumner, Dr. Oliver Wendell Holmes, Wendell Phillips, George S. Boutwell, Richard Henry Dana, Ralph Waldo Emerson, and Senator Thomas Hart Benton. The 1848–49 School Committee report commended the "remarkable order and stillness which have been manifested, week after week, in these large gatherings, composed, in a considerable proportion, of the youths of our schools . . .; we trust that, from all, an impulse has been given, friendly alike to intellectual, and social culture."[25]

Brighton was laying the foundation of its public library system in this period. The Brighton Social Library, a private association, was established in 1824. In 1856 it merged with a new society, the Brighton Library Association, which had been incorporated by the legislature for book circulation, public lectures, and exercises in debate, declamation, and composition. This was Brighton's first public library. It made its headquarters in the Town Hall.[26]

A rudimentary fire department also existed in the 1850s. By 1842 there were two engine houses, one in Brighton Center and the other in industrial North Brighton. The town relied on volunteer companies, which may well explain why three fire insurance companies maintained offices in Brighton.[27]

The 1850s also saw the establishment of the Brighton Avenue Baptist Church. There had been a handful of Baptists in Brighton from an early date. One of the founders of the Congregational Church Nathaniel Griggs, had urged the establishment of a Baptist Church as early as 1827.[28] Only in the 1850s, however, were the Baptists numerous enough to support a separate establishment. The first meeting of the new Baptist Society, held on October 21, 1855 in Union Hall at the intersection of Cambridge and North Beacon Streets, Union Square, was attended by just eleven persons. The first minister, the Reverend Joseph M. Graves, played a central role in organizing the congregation. In 1857 the handsome Brighton Avenue Baptist Church was built on the site of the present Union Square Fire Station.[29]

There was a major influx of Irish immigrants into Brighton in the late 1840s and 1850s, a phenomenon of enormous significance to the future of the community. Ireland experienced several successive failures of its potato crop, the dietary mainstay of the island, in these years. More than four-fifths of her population consisted of tenant farmers with just enough ground for a cottage and a small potato field. The potato rot which made its first appearance in 1845, subjected the country to a succession of miseries that has few parallels in modern history. Landlords drove the peasantry from their holdings. The years 1849 to 1851 were the most severe: one quarter of Ireland's farmers were displaced in these years. They immigrated, when they could, to Britain, Canada, and the United States. After falling off somewhat in the late 1850s, this immigration revived with the reappearance of the potato rot in 1863. By 1865 some two and a half million Irish had fled the country.[30]

The years 1845 to 1855 witnessed an enormous increase in the number of Irish Catholics residing in Brighton—a rise from 5 percent of the population to 35 percent in a single decade.[31] The town's convenience to Boston by highway and railroad, its cattle market, slaughterhouses, nurseries, and many small-scale industries served to attract Irish immigrants in substantial numbers.

The 1855 census shows the new element had three major characteristics. First, it was young. Seventy-nine percent of the Irish were under thirty years of age. Second, it was largely unmarried. Third, the vast majority were unskilled. Sixty percent listed their occupation as "laborer"; twenty-nine percent as "servant."[32]

Brighton's earliest Irish residents included Owen Callahan, who settled in the town before 1841 and lived near the Market and Faneuil Street intersection; Michael Coyle, a stonemason, father of eight children, who resided in Brighton as early as 1838 (one of his sons was later elected a state representative); William Ring who lived near Malbert Road, and who arrived before 1843; Hugh Fagan and James McNamara, both of whom resided near Union Square; James Carrigan, who lived on Eastburn Street (then called Worcester Street); Thomas Corcoran, in whose house on Eastburn Street the first Catholic Mass in Brighton was celebrated; also, Thomas Brennan and Patrick Tracey.[33]

Significantly, by 1854 seven of these early Irish residents had acquired a house of his own. Despite serious deficiencies of skills and capital, they made tangible gains over a relatively short span of years.[34]

Brighton's Irish population was at one and the same time concentrated and dispersed. The thirty percent employed as domestics, servants, and resident laborers by the wealthy of the town either lived in their employer's homes or in separate establishments in the vicinity of these residences. The majority, however, was clustered in three sections of the Town: (1) North Brighton, where they made up nearly fifty percent of the population; (2) the south side of Brighton Center, particularly Eastburn, Foster, Winship, and Shepard Streets; and (3) the Union Square area.[35]

Though most of the Irish were unskilled, they had come to an America that was never more the land of opportunity than in the second half of the nineteenth century. Laborers were needed to build new streets and aqueducts, sewerage, lighting, and transit systems, and residential, commercial, and public structures. While wages were low, employment was reliable. It was possible for a frugal family to maintain a tolerable standard of living while slowly accumulating savings for the purchase of property.

Anti-Irish feeling ran strong in Massachusetts in this period. The Protestant majority found Irish poverty, illiteracy, and Roman Catholicism offensive. As the numbers of Irish steadily mounted, these feelings intensified. In May 1854 a mob led by John S. Orr carried away a cross from a Catholic Church in Chelsea. In July of the same year a Catholic Church in Dorchester was blown up. In October 1854 *The Wide Awake*, a vituperative anti-Catholic and anti-Irish newspaper, made its appearance, thereafter providing a steady stream of anti-Papist literature. The political arm of the anti-Irish movement was the American, or Know Nothing Party, which gained power in 1854 by winning all but two of the seats in the

Massachusetts legislature, the entire congressional delegation, and by electing Henry J. Gardner as Governor. This victory had been described as "the most amazing political landslide in the history of the state."[36]

The Know Nothings ruled Massachusetts from 1855 to 1857. The support the voters of Brighton gave this anti-foreign movement provides an accurate measure of anti-Irish feelings in the Town. In 1854 the Know Nothing candidate for Governor polled sixty percent of the Brighton vote in a field of four candidates.[37] In other words, six out of ten Brighton voters favored a political program opposed to voting and officeholding privileges for Irish-Catholics. In 1855 Gardner again led a field of four candidates in Brighton, though his support had fallen to forty-two percent. He repeated this performance in the 1856 election. Only in his last, unsuccessful run for Governor in 1857 did he fail to top the ticket, running a near second in a field of three candidates with thirty-five percent. Nativist sentiment was clearly a powerful force in Brighton in the mid 1850s.

David Nevins, a wealthy manufacturer who owned Bellvue, an estate comprising the grounds of St. Elizabeth's Hospital and St. Gabriel's Monastery, was so fervently nativist in his sentiments that he refused to employ Irish as servants or laborers in any capacity. Once, when the roof of his mansion was leaking, and no Yankee workman could be found to make repairs, he chose to allow the rain to pour in rather than employ an Irish carpenter.[38]

Irish immigration led, in time, to the establishment of Brighton's first Catholic Church, St. Columbkille's. According to Thomas Muldoon, an early parishioner, prior to 1850 the Irish attended Father Flood's church in Watertown or other Catholic churches in Cambridge and Brookline. As previously noted, the first Mass took place in the home of Thomas Corcoran on Eastburn Street, sometime in the mid-1840s. Muldoon also recalled attend-

64

ing Mass in North Brighton in the homes of John Nolan on Waverly Street and Patrick Flynn on Western Avenue. In the early fifties Reverend P. O. Beire, Pastor of Roxbury's St. Joseph's Church, celebrated Mass in various houses in Brighton. In 1853 a lot on Bennett Street was purchased as a site for a church. While this structure was under construction, services were held in the loft of a barn owned by Albert Howe on the site of the present First National Bank on Chestnut Hill Avenue. "The loft was 45 feet long and 30 feet wide," Muldoon recalled, "with benches made of rough spruce boards, ten inches in width." The worshipers were "much disturbed by the jumping and prancing of horses and the barking and howling of dogs, in the stable beneath us. About 15 people attended Mass on Sundays."[39]

When St. Columbkille's opened in 1855, the priest in charge was Father Joseph Finotti, an Italian and a noted scholar. Father Finotti named the church for the Irish Saint Columba. The term "kille," which means church or monastery in Gaelic, had been attached to the saint's name in his lifetime in recognition of his eagerness to establish monasteries. The church, which stood near the northwest corner of Bennett and Market Streets, had a seating capacity of 675. It remained a mission district of Father Finotti's Brookline parish until 1871.[40]

Irish immigration also significantly influenced the politics of Brighton. Prior to the large-scale Irish influx, the town had been a Whig stronghold. As late as the 1848 to 1852 period, the Whigs commanded over sixty percent of the gubernatorial vote. The Democratic Party, dating from Andrew Jackson's presidency, had always been a distinct minority in Brighton. By the end of the decade of the 1850s, however, the Democrats, who actively recruited immigrant support, moved into a position of parity with the opposition, the recently founded Republican Party. Indicative of the changing political character was the response local authorities gave to the December 7, 1862 fire that totally destroyed St. Columbkille's Church. The Board of Selectmen offered Brighton Town Hall as a site for Catholic worhsip, an offer that the Catholics gratefully accepted. Regarding the auditorium where Saturday night dances were held to be unsuitable for the celebration of the Holy Mass, Father Finotti conducted services in a basement bordered on one side by a row of cells. Here the Catholics of Brighton met each week for the better part of a year while a new church was being constructed.[41]

CHAPTER VI

The Critical Years
1860-1880

The Town of Brighton marked its fiftieth anniversary on February 24, 1857 with appropriate exercises—the firing of a salute at noon, a ringing of church bells at sunset, and an evening fireworks display. Town Clerk William Warren summarized the progress of the town over the past half century as follows:

> Brighton when incorporated containing some five or six hundred inhabitants, now numbers near 3,000. At the time there was but one road communicating with Boston, making the distance through Roxbury over the neck so-called more than six miles. Now we have a choice of roads—the distance reduced to 3½ miles—or by railroad to fifteen minutes. Then we had but one church standing in front of the spot where the Unitarian meeting house now stands . . . . Now we have four churches, two of which have been erected during the last year. Then we had but two small schoolhouses, one in the building where I am now writing [Town Hall], and one in the easterly part of the town. Now we have five buildings . . . . These schools have about five hundred pupils regularly attending them being perfectly free to all where no distinction is made except that which naturally arises from superior and meritricious behavior. They are

attended with much expense, but the expense is freely bestowed—and they are the pride of the inhabitants as it is believed they are the safeguard of our happy institutions and on which more than any other thing will depend the perpetuation of those rights and that liberty which we now so freely enjoy.

Warren concluded his essay with a significant prediction. "It is hardly probable," he noted, "that this town will retain its corporate name for another half century for it may long before the expiration of that time be absorbed in the great commercial neighboring metropolis Boston."[1] When Warren resigned the clerkship later that year, he was replaced by his twenty-two year old son, the future congressman William Wirt Warren. In 1873 the younger Warren would make good on his father's prediction by securing legislative approval of a bill providing for the annexation of Brighton to the City of Boston.

The 1860 to 1880 period was one of far-reaching change for Allston-Brighton. It began with the great bloodletting of the Civil War. The town contributed large quantities of men, money, stores, and clothing to the war effort. It furnished 365 men, fifteen of whom were commissioned officers. Twenty-three of them met death, 12 in battle and 11 from the effects of disease. The women of the town likewise contributed significantly, furnishing clothing and army and hospital supplies under the auspices of the Soldiers Aid Society. Many Brighton women worked at the nearby Watertown Arsenal manufacturing arms and ammunition.[2]

Brighton welcomed its Civil War soldiers home on June 22, 1865 in a public celebration featuring a procession, the pealing of the bells, and the firing of cannon; a joyous ceremony, Frederick A. Whitney recounted, accompanied "by graceful decorations, by the smiles of mothers, by music and song, by feasting and dancing."[3]

The community did not, however, forget its war dead. Brighton was one of the first towns in Massachusetts to erect a soldier's monument. Paid for by the subscription of the townspeople, the thirty-foot tall granite obelisk was constructed on a rise of land at the center of Evergreen Cemetery, a site Whitney described as "thickly covered with forest trees." The Civil War monument was the work of George F. Meacham, designer of the Boston Public Gardens.[4]

The 1860s saw a marked decline in agriculture in Brighton. As the decade opened, the town contained 57 farms comprising 1,335 acres; sixty percent of its land was devoted to farming. By 1870 the number had fallen to a mere 27; only 21 percent of the town consisted of farms.[5]

The use of land for farming, even for the cultivation of high-priced market gardening and orchard products, became less profitable in the 1860s than the division of farms into building lots. The filling of Boston's Back Bay (a project begun in 1857) brought Brighton into the economic orbit of Boston. As streets were constructed and residences built in the Back Bay, the land in the adjoining community of Brighton took on increased desirability and value. Brighton's population increased by fifty percent in the 1860 to 1870 period, rising from 3,375 to 4,970.[6]

The 1866 to 1870 period saw the building of the Chestnut Hill Reservoir, the largest public works project in the history of Allston-Brighton. Prior to its construction, Boston's water supply, which came from Lake Cochituate in Framingham, had been stored in four small reservoirs in Brookline, on Beacon Hill, and South Boston and East Boston. In 1859 a major break in the system left the city with just four days supply of water. This emergency prompted the Cochituate Water Works Board to recommend the construction of a much larger storage facility near Boston.

A shortage of capital and manpower during the Civil

War delayed the project. In 1865, however, the Water Works Board purchased a 212-acre property on the Brighton-Newton boundary for the new facility. The parcel included much of Brighton's Waugh estate (formerly the farm of Benjamin Baker). Beacon Street, which passed through the center of the property, was re-routed to the east. A meadow belonging to Amos Lawrence of the famous textile manufacturing family was also acquired. Lawrence's home stood on the heights above this meadow where Boston College stands today.[7]

Several Brighton residents played significant roles in the construction of the reservoir. The contract for teaming went to Benjamin Franklin Ricker and George A. Wilson of Brighton. Ricker owned the largest livery stable in the city of Boston, located on School Street. Wilson, who operated the Brighton Hotel, was a major property owner and real estate promoter.[8] In October 1868 their firm had 88 teams working at the reservoir. Some $474,000 was paid to the Ricker and Wilson firm by the Water Works Board for this work, a sum representing twenty percent of the total cost of the project. At its height the reservoir project furnished employment for nearly 800 workers.[9] Many of them settled in Brighton on a permanent basis.

Another Brighton resident, William Henry Jackson, joined the project's engineering staff in 1868. In later years, while serving as Boston City Engineer, Jackson supervised the construction of the Longfellow and Harvard Bridges across the Charles River.[10]

The building of the reservoir also led to a boundary change. In 1875, a short time after the annexation of Brighton by Boston, the boundary line between Brighton and Newton was redrawn so as to place the entire reservoir within the city of Boston. Newton was compensated by an altered boundary north of the reservoir, extending from the smaller or Lawrence Basin to a point on the Charles River about a quarter of a mile east of the original boundary. This transfer gave Newton about a hundred acres of prime real estate on Washington Hill.[11]

In 1869 Boston attorney Uriel H. Crocker proposed a grandiose plan for the creation of a park that would extend from the vicinity of the present Boston University Bridge to the Chestnut Hill Reservoir. Corey Hill was to be the central element in this reservation, that eminence affording, Crocker noted, "the finest view of Boston and the neighboring cities and towns, of the harbor and of the country for miles around, that is to be obtained in this vicinity—a view upon the beauties of which it is useless to enlarge, but which must be seen to be appreciated." Such a park, Crocker asserted, would be "superior to Central Park of New York." It is fascinating to speculate on the impact the creation of such a park would have had on the subsequent development of Allston-Brighton.[12]

With the growth in population, new religious societies were formed. In 1861 a Universalist Church was built on Cambridge Street on the site of the present Allston Knights of Columbus Hall. One of its ministers, the Reverend Thomas W. Silloway, was a noted architect who designed the Vermont State House and an estimated four hundred New England churches in the course of a long and distinguished career. Silloway resigned the post of minister in 1867 to devote his full energies to architecture. He continued as a resident of Allston until his death in 1910.[13] The Brighton Universalist Church was short lived, closing its doors in 1887.

An Episcopal congregation was organized in 1854 by the Reverend Cyrus F. Knight, a native son, who later served as Episcopal Bishop of Milwaukee.[14] In 1864 the Episcopalians built the Church of the Epiphany, a handsome wooden Gothic Revival structure at the corner of Washington and Eastburn Streets. In 1872 it was sold to a new parish under the name of St. Margaret's Church.[15]

The Brighton Congregationalist Church acquired a new

and expanded building in 1868, the work of George F. Fuller, son of Granville A. Fuller, architect of the Brighton Town Hall. The younger Fuller, who graduated from Yale, received many important commissions in the course of a long and distinguished career.[16]

A Methodist Church was organized in Brighton in 1872. The church structure, dating from 1876, still stands at the corner of Harvard Avenue and Farrington Street in Allston.[17]

By 1871 the Catholic population of Brighton had grown to such an extent that Archbishop John Williams authorized the construction of the present St. Columbkille's Church. The largest of Brighton's churches was built in three widely separated stages on a design attributed to a "Mr. O'Connor." The present lower church dated from 1875. The upper floor was completed on July 4, 1880, at which point the parish had some two thousand members. The Italianate tower was not added until the turn of the century and contrasts with the Victorian Gothic style of the body of the church. There is a striking resemblance between St. Columbkille's Church and the ruined Cathedral of Iona which was established by St. Columbkille.[18]

With the filling of Boston's Back Bay, the relatively sparsely settled eastern end of Brighton began to develop. Prior to 1867 there was no railroad depot in Allston. A tiny cobbler's shop occupied the site. The cobbler kept a few tickets in a box and would occasionally flag down a train for a traveller.[19] The intersection of Cambridge Street and Harvard Avenue was known as Cambridge Crossing, a name that confused travellers who would sometimes stop there thinking they were in Cambridge only to discover that it was over a mile away.[20] In 1867 a wooden depot was constructed. Years later a letter appearing in the *Brighton Item* signed "W" (possibly written by J.P.C. Winship) explained the choice of the name Allston for the area.

February 11, 1868 an informal meeting was called at the station then named Cambridge Crossing, to consider the subject of a new Post Office for that section of the town: of course the matter of the name had to be decided. The meeting was adjourned to the next evening when individuals marked for a name and by a suggestion of Rev. F. A. Whitney, who was not present, Allston was talked of and finally selected. Subsequently the name was approved by the Postmaster-general at Washington and April 7 of the same year the Allston Post Office was opened to the public. Furthermore, the Superintendent of the Boston & Albany Railroad issued an order that "on and after June 1, 1868, the station now known as Cambridge Crossing shall be called Allston. Mr. Whitney's reasons for advocating the name were that the great painter lived and died in Cambridge, hardly a mile away from some parts of the district, and that Brighton was, from the settlement of the country down to 1807, a part of Cambridge. Among the other names suggested was West Longwood, but the objection was raised that there was already one Longwood on a branch road and a second might cause confusion . . . . There never was a town of Allston— it was merely a postal station of the Brighton District, and a railroad station.[21]

The town contained over forty small slaughterhouses which in 1869 handled 53,000 cattle, 342,000 sheep, and 144,000 hogs. The slaughterhouses had been the economic mainstay of the community for the better part of a century. In 1860 they represented a capital investment of $542,000, furnished more than 200 jobs, and produced over $4 million in meat and animal by-products—chiefly beef, pork, mutton, veal, lard, hides, pelts, and tallow.[22] Their operations, however, were carried on with little regard to public health.

Fearing an outbreak of cholera in Brighton in 1866, the local Board of Health hired Dr. Henry Clark to investigate the problem. Brighton contained 42 slaughterhouses in 1866, concentrated chiefly along Western Avenue, Cambridge Street, the eastern end of Washington Street, and in the Chestnut Hill Avenue and Foster Street section south of Brighton Center. Proximity to a stream or pond, into which blood and refuse could be emptied, was an important factor in the choice of these locations. The Clark report noted that the establishments were "conducted in a manner which I consider both disagreeable and dangerous, directly and remotely, to the immediate vicinity, and to public and individual health." He went on to cite the establishments of the Jacksons, Brown and Rogers, Dyer and Frost, Curtis and Boynton, Jeremiah Pratt, and Timothy and Stephen Brooks for particular censure.[23]

The Brooks brother's establishment, which was situated between Chestnut Hill Avenue and Foster Street, he noted, "was discharging its semi-liquid filth all over the ground, directly in the rear, which after mixing with water in a little pond, took its course northerly through or near Baxter's Place, thence by Osborne's to George Brooks', and thence through Nonantum Vale and into Charles River." The Faneuil Valley Brook, a system of natural streams and ponds, carried away the discharge. Dr. Clark described this method of disposal as "prolific and provoking causes of disease," and recommended that foul matter instead be buried or neutralized, that offal be carried away in tightly closed carts, and that the town prohibit the keeping of swine where they might feed on "such disgusting food."[24]

Despite an assertion in the next year's town report that Dr. Clark's recommendations had been carried out voluntarily by the slaughterhouse proprietors, conditions did not improve.[25] By 1869 the Massachusetts Board of Health

74

affirmed that polluted air from the Brighton slaughter-houses was "familiar to all who pass the Allston Station on the Albany Railroad in the summer months or who drive through the town on the common roads. It is perceptible on the other side of Charles River, in Cambridge, when the wind blows in that direction."[26]

Disposal of the unusable portion of the slaughtered animals was the key problem.

The great source of offence in all these establishments [the report read] consists in the manner of disposing of the parts of the animal used neither for food nor in the arts. In the ox these parts are, the larger portion of the intestines and all of their contents, the "omasum" or third stomach, the spleen, the lungs and about half of the blood. In the sheep, the intestines, spleen, stomach and all of the blood. Every slaughterhouse has a piggery, into which are thrown all these portions of the cattle and the sheep. The result is a putrid mass, consisting of blood, which decomposes almost as soon as it falls upon such material, the excrement of the animals killed, and of the hogs, the half digested food contained in the entrails, and the offal itself, covered with decomposing matter. In this filth the hogs wallow. At uncertain intervals it is scraped and banked up on the ground (often very spongy), to await a purchaser, or is carted off to be spread upon land. The track of these carts is evident, on the roads, both to sight and smell. The fat is carted for long distances in various directions, a portion going to Roxbury, another to Watertown, another to Cambridge and elsewhere. The portion of the blood of cattle which does not go to the hogs is taken away for sugar refiners, but often not until it has become disgustingly putrid. The floors of the slaughterhouses are of wood, and are saturated with

75

blood. In most of them there is no sewerage; generally an imperfect drain leads to some marsh or low piece of ground; sometimes to a brook. The surrounding ground is filled with decomposing matter.[27]

Of 120 deaths in Brighton in 1869, forty-one were attributable to its town's unhealthy slaughtering practices. A scarlet fever epidemic took fifteen lives; the whooping cough claimed another ten victims; typhoid fever was responsible for the death of another six; diptheria another four. Over ninety percent of the victims were children under the age of thirteen, a consequence the State Board of Health had predicted.[28] "If anything is settled as to the causes of disease," its report read, "it is the influence of decomposing organic matter in giving rise to diarrhoeal [sic] affections and typhoid fever, in depressing the vitality of children, thus rendering them less capable of resisting disease in every form, and in making all the epidemics more active and virulent."[29]

These conditions provided a rationale for the Legislature's 1870 incorporation of the Butcher's Slaughtering and Melting Association with the exclusive right to slaughter cattle within a six-mile radius of Boston. In 1872 a second act gave the Brighton Board of Selectmen licensing power over the local butchering activities.[30]

The bill to create the Butcher's Slaughtering and Melting Association, or Brighton Abattoir, was presented to the Massachusetts Legislature by State Senator William Wirt Warren of Brighton. The incorporators were members of the Brighton Board of Selectmen, Horace W. Baxter, Horace W. Jordan, and Benjamin Franklin Ricker —all three leading butchers. The legislature's creation of the Abattoir gave these Brighton men an effective monopoly over the slaughtering industry in the Boston area. Their rivals accused them of driving competitors to the wall by means fair or foul. They also charged that the

State Board of Health was in league with the Brighton interests. "The whole story," asserted the attorney for the rival group in testimony before a legislative committee, "there is no disguising it, no use varnishing over, is that these men forming this single corporation want to do all the slaughtering business in Brighton and vicinity, and kill every other man out; and that the Board of Health fraternize, and join hands, and sympathize with them."[31]

William Wirt Warren was thirty-six years of age in 1870 when he guided the abattoir bill through the legislature. A graduate of Harvard and an attorney, he had been associated with Brighton town government since succeeding his father as Town Clerk in 1857. Winship described Warren as a "power" in the town. He rose to a position of influence in the affairs of the Massachusetts Democratic Party, serving as local Collector of Internal Revenue, as State Senator, candidate for state Attorney General and Congressman.[32]

The year 1870, which marked Warren's election to the State Senate, also saw a major shift in the political leadership of Brighton, for in that year the Board of Selectmen fell under the control of Baxter, Ricker, and Jordan.[33] In 1872 Patrick Moley, the first Irishman to win election as a selectman, replaced Baxter, who moved to the Board of Assessors. These men may be said to have effectively dominated the political life of Brighton in the last four years of its existence as an independent town.[34]

In 1876 the *Boston Daily Advertiser* published an editorial entitled "A Specimen Reformer," charging William Wirt Warren and his associates with systematically robbing the Town of Brighton in the years before annexation.

The Brighton Ring was, in its way, as dishonest and avaricious a political association as the Tammany Ring in New York. It burdened the little town with an enormous debt, and the people were driven to desire annexation for relief from its exactions.

Its method of operations was to buy on account of the town parcels of real estate belonging to democrats at exorbitant prices, even for the times, when the value of property was most inflated. One schoolhouse lot and engine-house lot were bought. The last speculation of the kind was the purchase of a hotel property not wanted for any purpose. It belonged to a prominent Democrat, and was worth perhaps $40,000. Mr. Warren was one of the responsible men in these transactions, although he commonly avoided direct interference himself. The purchase of this hotel property, however, was such a palpable fraud that one Democrat, an Irishman, revolted and declined to do the part alloted to him in the business.

In this exigency Mr. Warren's vote was required to accomplish the scheme, and he was under such pressure and obligations that he could not refuse it. His vote was given for the infamous transaction by which about $80,000 was paid by the town to a member of the ring, for property not then worth more than half the amount, and which could hardly be sold today for $25,000, and has never been needed for public purposes. The Republicans of Brighton, and the honest Democrats as well, have a very poor opinion of Mr. Warren's claim to be a reformer. They remember that in small things affecting their local interests he was unfaithful . . . .[35]

While the *Daily Advertiser* editorial was highly partisan, written at the height of Warren's unsuccessful congressional reelection campaign, strong circumstantial evidence supports its allegations. When the so-called Brighton Ring came to power in 1870, the town's debt stood at a rather modest $89,000; by 1874, the year Brighton was annexed to Boston, the debt had risen to $713,000, an eightfold increase in just four years. Moreover, spending greatly exceeded income in the 1870 to 1873 period. The town collected less than $500,000 in revenue, but spent $1.56 million, three times its income. It made up the difference by borrowing over a million dollars.[36]

With the establishment of the Brighton Abattoir, a major obstacle to the development of the town had been removed; but a second, equally challenging impediment remained. Many parts of Brighton, particularly the more elevated central and western sections of the town, were relatively inaccessible to those with jobs in Boston. The town as a whole, moreover, was lacking in good roads, sewerage, and street lighting, which were then as now the prerequisites of large-scale development.[37] Many of the expenditures of the 1870 to 1873 period were unquestionably justified. About one third of the money, for example, went for road construction and the installation of sewers. The town's topography—its many hills, marshes, and mudflats—presented serious drainage problems. It is the sheer scale of the spending, however, that surprises. Was there a Brighton Ring?

The strongest bit of evidence supporting the *Daily Advertiser's* charges was the town's 1873 purchase of the Brighton Hotel from George A. Wilson, a business associate of Selectman Ricker. According to the town records, the hotel property was purchased as the site for a new town hall.[38] Inasmuch as annexation to Boston was a foregone conclusion, one may well ask what need the town had for such a facility. The $75,000 price the town paid for the property, moreover, was extremely high. Two years earlier the Catholics of Brighton had acquired a substantially larger parcel of land for their new church on a nearby street for a modest $6,400.[39] In 1874, the very year of annexation, a member of the Boston Board of Aldermen charged that the Brighton Hotel property would not bring half its purchase price on the open market. He demanded an investigation of the transaction, but the matter was quietly tabled.[40] The *Brighton Messenger* alluded to the charges on its editorial page in January 1874, only to dismiss the matter as "hardly worth while . . . now that the change in the government of Brighton has been fully accomplished."[41]

Annexation commanded the active support of Warren and his associates. On January 10, 1872 the town established a committee to remonstrate with the Massachusetts Legislature and the Boston City Council for annexation. The five-man body included Warren, Ricker, and Jordan.[42] On January 25, 1872 a pro-annexation petition, initiated by George A. Wilson, was filed with the legislature.[43] Wilson served as the first state representative after annexation. In February the legislature heard the opponents of annexation. Leading this group was Abiel F. Rice, a North Brighton strawberry farmer.[44] The struggle between the pro and anti-annexation forces came to a head at a December 1872 town meeting, when by an 84 to 62 vote the town authorized the expenditure of "such sums of money as may be necessary" to cover the expenses of the Selectmen in promoting the annexation cause.[45] The annexation bill passed the legislature in May 1873.

The annexation question was put to the voters of Brighton on October 7, 1873. "Shall an act," the ballot question read, "of the Legislature of this Commonwealth in the year eighteen hundred seventy-three, entitled 'An Act to Unite the City of Boston and the Town of Brighton' be accepted?" By a vote of 622 to 133 the townspeople answered in the affirmative.[46] Three months later, on the first Monday of January 1874, Brighton became a part of the City of Boston.[47]

Allston-Brighton benefitted from the union with Boston. The local police force, for example, was expanded from just four officers working exclusively at night except for Market Day to twenty-one men, one for every 209

80

The Holton Library, built in 1874, stood on the site of the present Brighton Branch of the Boston Public Library on Academy Hill Road. To its right is the Nathaniel Jackson House, now on Winship Street.

Brighton residents.[48] Within five years two new grammar schools, a handsome new public library, and a new engine house were opened by the city. In 1874 the Bennett Grammar School, which had been housed since 1861 in a wooden structure on the site of the present Winship School, moved to a modern brick building on Chestnut Hill Avenue. Its namesake, Stephen Hastings Bennett, a leading Brighton cattleman, had donated the lot on which the original building stood.[49] The Allston Grammar School, situated on Cambridge Street near Harvard Avenue, opened in 1879. In 1893 its name was changed to the Washington Allston Grammar School.[50]

The new library stood on Academy Hill Road on the site of the present Brighton Branch Library. This Victorian Gothic structure, designed by George Fuller, cost a substantial $70,000. It was named for James Holton, who left Brighton a bequest in 1863 for the support of its library. Both the Bennett School and the Holton Library were under construction at the time of annexation. Thus, as Walter Muir Whitehill noted of the Brighton Branch Library, these structurs were "acquired, almost ready made, by process of municipal accretion."[51]

The last major structure to be built in this period was a new fire station on Chestnut Hill Avenue.

With annexation came a loss of local self-determination. In 1879 the Boston School Committee proposed closing Brighton High School. Benjamin F. Paine, a local merchant, led the fight to save the school. The issue was ultimately resolved in the town's favor, the official public record of the School Committee noting that "petitions, numerously signed, have been presented, remonstrating against the discontinuance of the school, and a large delegation of the leading citizens of Brighton have borne strong testimony to its utility, and have urged that its discontinuance would be a serious injury to the welfare of that section of the city.[52] This struggle gave Allston-Brighton a foretaste of the many battles it would be obliged to wage in the years ahead against a government that would grow increasingly arbitrary and remote.

CHAPTER VII

Streetcar Suburb

1880–1915

The 1880 to 1915 period was one of greatly accelerated growth for Allston-Brighton. Improvements in transportation were a major factor in this growth. Already by the 1860s and 1870s a few residents were regularly commuting to Boston by train. While the depots at Allston Square, North Brighton, and Faneuil were within easy commuting distance of the city, working-class people could not afford the high fares. The introduction of a horse railway service in the late 1870s generated additional growth, but this mode of travel was relatively slow and inconvenient. It was only with the coming of electric streetcars in the late 1880s that large-scale residential development was feasible. As Sam Bass Warner, Jr. noted of this phenomenon, "In the late 1880s and 1890s the electrification of street railways brought convenient transportation to at least the range of six miles from City Hall. The rate of building and settlement in the period became so rapid that the whole scale and plan of Greater Boston was entirely made over."[1] Property values along the streetcar route appreciated. In the half century between 1880 and 1915 Allston-Brighton's population shot up from 6,700 to over 30,000.

The revolution in land use had begun as early as the 1860s with the sale and subdivision of several large farms. In 1881 the Brighton Stockyards, which had stood to the rear of the Cattle Fair Hotel since the early years of the century, were moved to a site on North Beacon Street in

North Brighton, a location convenient both to the recently constructed Brighton Abattoir and to the Brighton Depot.[2] The local slaughtering industry was in decline by the 1880s. With the introduction of refrigerated railroad cars in the 1870s, long distance meat shipment became possible. This effectively undercut the local industry. After 1880 the Brighton facility concentrated largely on the production of kosher meats, which Judaic law stipulated had to be eaten within seventy-two hours of slaughtering.[3] In addition to bringing several Jewish butchers to the Abattoir, the industry attracted a dozen or so Jewish families to North Brighton, including a Rabbi, the Reverend Moses Katkoff. The Abattoir likewise drew Lithuanian and Polish workers into the neighborhood.[4] The Lithuanian Cooperative Association on Lincoln Street was a social focal point of North Brighton in the first half of the century. Immigration historian Philip Taylor has noted how "each ethnic group felt the need to organize its own welfare institutions, the transaction of whose business also met the need for social life."[5]

With the removal of the stockyards from Brighton Center, a valuable parcel was available for residential development. The architecture of the north side of Brighton Center is uniformly late Victorian owing to the 1881 removal of the stockyards.

The facility left its imprint on the area in another respect: the elaborate residences which important cattle dealers constructed nearby. Examples include the Stephen Hastings Bennett house on Market Street; the William Munroe house on Malbert Road; the James Stetson house (now the McNamara Funeral Home) on Washington Street; and the Abram Collins house on Oakland Street. The most elaborate of the cattle dealer residences, however, and the last to be constructed was the James A. Hathaway mansion at the corner of Chestnut Hill Avenue and Dighton Street, dating from 1897.[6]

In 1872 Hathaway had formed a partnership with Gustavus Franklin Swift, who was later to found the Swift Meatpacking Company in Chicago. Swift had already established himself as a successful cattle dealer when Hathaway invited him to join his firm as a buyer. Swift lived in Brighton only very briefly in the early 1870s. The responsibilities of a buyer required that he follow the source of supply westward, first to Albany, then to Buffalo, and finally in 1874, to Chicago. The partnership was dissolved in 1877, when Hathaway rejected Swift's proposal that the firm engage in the year-round shipment of beef to eastern markets in refrigerated cars, an innovative idea destined to revolutionize the meatpacking industry.[7] While Swift built a fortune estimated at $12 million in Chicago, Hathaway prospered more modestly in Brighton exporting western cattle to European markets. In 1898 alone he shipped 90,000 head of cattle to agents in Liverpool, England.[8]

Rising land values led to the subdivision of other parcels. The old Sparhawk estate was surveyed for residential development by Edward Corey Sparhawk as early as 1873. It was not until the 1880s, however, following the installation of electric streetcars, that the area experienced significant development.

Boston's first electric streetcars began operating on January 1, 1889 along a route running from Park Square, by way of Boylston Street, Massachusetts Avenue, Beacon Street, Coolidge Corner, and Harvard Street to a stationhouse on Braintree Street in Allston. A branch of this line also ran from Coolidge Corner to the Chestnut Hill Reservoir. A third branch was soon after opened linking the line to Oak Square via Washington Street. The West End Street Railway Company, which operated these lines, was a major owner of Beacon Street real estate. The lines were built primarily to facilitate the development of Beacon Street. Large-scale residential development of

Allston-Brighton began with the introduction of electric streetcar service.[9]

The Gardner Street area south of the Allston Depot offers a graphic example of the impact these transportation improvements had on local development. In 1875 this neighborhood of about 65 acres, situated a few stops from the Allston Depot, contained a mere 31 residences. By 1885 the number had risen to 101; by 1890 it totalled 175. This was residential development, moreover, of a high order. In 1900 Gardner-Linden-Chester street section of South Allston was one of Boston's prestigious neighborhoods.

Several South Allston landmarks were constructed during these years. In 1887 the Boston & Albany Railroad replaced its wooden depot with the present Romanesque Revival structure designed by Shepley, Rutan and Coolidge, the successor firm to H. H. Richardson.[11] The adjacent Allston Hall block was built in 1889 by Samuel Hano, a local book manufacturer whose factory was situated a short distance away on Hano Street. Hano also built row houses on Hano, Blaine, and Everett Streets for his own employees and those of the Boston & Albany repair shops and the Sewall & Day Cordage Works in North Allston. At the height of his career, he owned more than a million dollars of South Allston real estate. When he declared bankruptcy in 1891, following the destruction of his factory by fire, the *Item* declared Hano had shown "a push and decision seldom equaled" which "had guided to completion building after building and utilized to the best possible advantage acre upon acre of land which five years ago had but a very small value in comparison."[12]

A fire station was built on Harvard Avenue in 1891 (too late, unfortunately, to save Hano's factory).[13] In 1893 the Chester Block, named for developer W. R. Chester, was constructed on Cambridge Street between Franklin and Wilton Streets, adjacent to the depot. This structure was designed by the noted church architect, Franz Joseph Untersee, who also designed St. Anthony's Church in North Allston.[14]

Horse racing was a popular diversion in the 19th century, but not an especially profitable one. Thus Beacon Park Raceway, which had occupied a 50-acre parcel of land on the east side of lower Cambridge Street since 1864, was purchased by the Boston & Albany Railroad in the 1890s and converted to a freight yard. A roundhouse and other railroad structures were built at the location.[15]

The community's preoccupation with development led to a 1903 proposal that its name be changed from Brighton to Allston Heights on the grounds that the older name was associated with the unpleasant slaughtering industry and would discourage potential real estate buyers.[16]

Another event reflecting Allston-Brighton's rapid development was the establishment in late 1885 of the *Item*. According to the Union List of Newspapers, a guide to American newspapers, the first paper to appear in Brighton was the *Mercury*, published very briefly in 1851. In 1860 two more papers made a fleeting appearance, the *Reporter* and the *Gem*. Then in 1871 came a more successful journal, the *Messenger*, which survived for five years. By the mid-eighties Brighton was more than ready for a weekly paper.

The *Item's* founder was George Warren, a nephew of William Wirt Warren, who left Boston Latin School in his junior year to establish the paper, which he edited until his death in 1944.[17]

The late 1880s and early 1890s witnessed the construction through Allston-Brighton of a major new roadway, Commonwealth Avenue. A group of six Boston businessmen, including Allston resident Isaac Pratt, Jr., were behind this key development project. They proposed to build a 200-foot-wide roadway with a central park and bridle path, flanked by macadamized driveways. Anticipating large profits from increased property values, two of the promoters, Charles Francis Adams and Ebenezer Francis, offered to give the land for the avenue, pointing out, as the *Item* reported on August 7, 1886, "that the proposed changes lie completely within the city and that the land to be taken is owned by only four businessmen."[18]

Since the city delayed approving the proposal, Commonwealth Avenue was not completed until after the construction in 1887 of Beacon Street in Brookline. "Economic justification of the undertaking was prompt and convincing," wrote Brookline historian John Gould Curtis. Within six years strips of land running back 500 feet from Beacon Street had increased in assessed valuation by $4.5 million. Land values in Brookline were booming. Development of a highly desirable nature was proceeding apace.[19]

The construction of Commonwealth Avenue began in 1892 as Beacon Street reached completion. The projected avenue, like Beacon Street planned by renowned landscape architect Frederick Law Olmsted, passed through one of Allston-Brighton's least developed areas; so underdeveloped, in fact, that sportsmen from Boston sometimes visited it to hunt quail and pheasant. Few buildings had to be moved or demolished along the route. It did, however, present some construction problems. A sizeable swamp near Harvard Avenue had to be filled and ledge outcroppings had to be cut back at several points.[20]

Some development had already occurred at the southern end of the avenue in the Aberdeen section. The proximity of the Beacon Street streetcar line made this a convenient residential neighborhood. In 1890 the *Item* listed the advantages of the Aberdeen section of Brighton: "Several feet above any considerable portion of land in the neighborhood, commanding magnificent views in every direction, well-watered, a perfect combination of woodland, and glade, and admitting the free exercise of the artistic taste of the landscape gardner [sic], these lands are sure to be sought for residential purposes by the most desirable buyers."[21] The Aberdeen developers were very careful to take advantage of the natural contours of the land in laying out streets. The dominant architectural styles were romantic, the Jacobethan, Queen Anne, and Shingle predominating.[22] The streets were given English and Scottish Shire names such as Lanark, Selkirk, Sutherland, and Orkney.

The developers of Commonwealth Avenue were to be sadly disappointed in their expectation of rapid development, however. Beacon Street offered potential developers many more advantages than Commonwealth Avenue—its earlier completion, proximity to Boston, and the active cooperation of local officials eager to make the avenue one of the great residential thoroughfares of Greater Boston. By contrast, progress on Commonwealth Avenue was slow. Then, just as the roadway reached completion, the Depression of 1893 struck, severely damaging the real estate market. Only two structures of significance were built on the avenue before 1900: an imposing stone residence near Mount Hood Road, built for cattle dealer William Munroe (now the Hasiotis Funeral Home) and the Princeton Hotel at the corner of Spofford Street near Harvard Avenue. The latter, an apartment building, remains one of the Avenue's handsomest structures.

Cynthia Zaitzevsky, a recent biographer of Olmsted, has noted that the avenue's construction "proceeded very slowly, and the planting of street trees was delayed until well after the turn of the century. Consequently, real estate development was diverted to Brookline, where Beacon Street was being constructed with much more dispatch."[23] Only five more apartment buildings were constructed prior to 1910. Full scale development did not come to Commonwealth Avenue until the 1910 to 1925 period.[24]

The inadequacies of the old high school on Academy Hill Road were universally recognized. A student satire, published in the 1891 graduation program, made the point.

It was built many years ago and is now nearly past use except as kindling wood . . . . It is chilled by a very nice furnace which gives off no heat under any circumstances in winter until 11:30 a.m. and is used as an ice cream freezer in the summer. On the first floor are laboratories and algebra rooms; the latter is the best place in the City of Boston to obtain a fine sample of pneumonia. Upstairs is a large room filled with so many desks that the teachers and scholars have to be trained acrobats in order to reach the blackboards. Also a miniature library and office . . . . These are only a few of the charms and advantages the Brighton High School has over other schools but are these not enough to show the need of a new school building?[25]

While all agreed that a new building was needed, a long and vociferous debate raged over the most appropriate site for the facility. Many favored the Academy Hill lot.[26] The *Item* cited "the fine air and extensive view," when it editorialized in favor of keeping the high school at its hilltop location.[27] The principal argument against the site was its remoteness. J.C.P. Winship, the community's representative on the School Committee, recommended a site on Cambridge Street, east of Mount St. Joseph's Academy.[28] A corner lot at the intersection of Cambridge and Warren Streets was ultimately selected. The chief drawback to this site was its nearness to Beatty's Ledge, a quarry on the site of Kennedy Memorial Hospital. There were several quarries in the town at the height of the development era when stone, gravel, and sand were in

90

Washington Allston School.

high demand. Another large one existed on Brock Street (McMurtry's Ledge).[29]

The new high school (now the Taft Middle School) was constructed in 1894 from a design by City Architect Edmund March Wheelwright. In his 1894 annual report, Wheelwright asserted that Brighton High School featured "architectural treatment involving increased expense throughout the entire structure" and that it was "much better built than many school buildings elsewhere in the state outside of Boston." Wheelwright was one of the leading municipal architects of his day.[30]

Since annexation in 1874 the old town hall had served as Allston-Brighton's municipal courthouse and police station. By the 1890s the community outgrew the facility. It took several years to win city approval of the construction of a new police station. Alderman John Lee led the fight to locate it on the site of the old Brighton Hotel. With the demolition of the hotel in 1889, the property had come into the hands of the Boston Street Department and was being used for the storage of equipment and supplies, creating an eyesore that lowered local real estate values.

Recent extensive movements in real estate have completely changed the appearance of the large tract between Sparhawk and Henshaw streets, the *Item* editorialized in late 1891, and much depends on the attention given the section intervening between Washington Street. Residences of a very high class have already been built to a considerable extent, and it is undoubtedly a fact that the uncertainty regarding the final disposition of the old Wilson Hotel estate has caused many would be buyers and improvers of property to hesitate before making a move in this excellent neighborhood.[31]

In 1893 the city gave way to mounting public pressure and constructed a handsome Classical Revival police station on the site. Station 14, like the new Brighton High School, was designed by City Architect Wheelwright. The Sparhawk Street area to the rear of the Police Station soon became one of the finest residential neighborhoods in Boston. By 1900 large-scale late Victorian residences lined Menlo, Sparhawk, and Murdock Streets. Mapleton Street experienced similar development a decade later.[32] Samuel N. Davenport, an architect and builder who resided at 19–21 Sparhawk Street, played a major role in the emergence of this distinguished neighborhood.[33]

Concerns for the preservation of open spaces for recreational purposes frequently accompanies large-scale development. Earlier in the century the people of Brighton had recreational access to many open fields and wooded lots. J.P.C. Winship owned a large parcel of land called "Winship's Woods," off Chestnut Hill Avenue south to Wallingford Road, that was used for the annual Unitarian Sunday School picnic.[34]

By the 1890s the amount of open land in which such events could occur, while by no means exhausted, was nonetheless rapidly diminishing. The *Item* noted in an editorial of March 8, 1890: "We have a fountain, a plot from which much care is taken to exclude the boys during ball time, and it has been customary to hire a lot of land near the railroad for baseball and playground purposes. This is the extent of parks in Brighton."[35]

While there was general consensus that the community needed a playground, and the city agreed to purchase land, the question of location generated prolonged controversy. There was no problem selecting a name; it would be called Rogers Park, after Hiram Rogers, the President of the Boston Board of Aldermen, a leading resident of Allston.[36]

The first location proposed was a parcel of land adjacent to the West End Street Railway carbarns in Oak Square. This proposal raised a storm of opposition, however. The site was objected to on the grounds that it was far removed from the center of the community; that the land, which belonged to Horace Brackett, was overpriced; and that the proposed site was low and swampy and would be expensive to improve.[37]

The effect a park would have on the value of surrounding residential property was recognized by real estate owners. Oak Square property owners strongly favored the proposed location. Residents of other sections of the community were equally determined, however, that it be

93

situated elsewhere. Ultimately the city resorted to advertising for land.[38] A number of parcels were offered, and following a visit to each location by the Mayor and a delegation of city officials, the present Rogers Park site was selected.[39] It is interesting that the choice fell upon a six and a half acre property belonging to Henry B. Goodenough, a member of the Boston City Council. One wonders if politics played a part in the decision. In announcing the decision, the *Item* observed that "nothing has caused so much excitement for years as the struggle for the location of this park."[40]

Other parks would be established over the next half century, but with much less controversy. Smith Playground in North Allston was the second park established. It was laid out in the 1890s. Then, in the 1909 to 1916 period, three more were added: the Ringer Playground on Allston Street; the Chestnut Hill Playground at Cleveland Circle; and the Portsmouth Street Playground in North Brighton.[41]

Allston-Brighton's landscape was literally transformed in these years. Four major brooks, numerous lesser streams, and a dozen small ponds were drained, filled, or diverted by developers. "In this district more abuses of the natural water-courses, in the way of obstruction, obliteration, and connection with the sewers, has taken place than in any other part of the city," noted the 1894 Boston Street Department Annual Report.[42] The same report recommended that they be developed in the manner of the Fenway "with their banks terraced and planted with shady trees and flowering shrubs, with well-designed stone-arched bridges; til the whole effect is most charming to those who admire landscape."[43] Since no steps were taken to carry through the recommended improvements, haphazard development continued; and by 1930 the natural system of streams and ponds was almost totally destroyed—the ponds mostly drained and the brooks and streams filled or buried in conduits.

A much happier fate awaited another major natural feature, Allston-Brighton's Charles River frontage. The river had once been a splendid scenic resource. Henry Wadsworth Longfellow had written of "the bright and free meadows" of Brighton. By the 1890s, however, the river was lined with wharves, warehouses, and industrial facilities and was spanned in its Allston-Brighton secion of four and a half miles by five drawbridges. In addition, it had become a serious threat to public health.[44] "The upper portion received the discharge from public sewers in Brighton and much refuse matter from the Abattoir, and the lower portion the discharge from many public sewers in Cambridge," an 1894 sanitary report noted. "The amount of upland water was not large enough to dilute this great amount of polluting matter so as to make it inoffensive; and as the amount of water decreases with the distance up stream, the water in the upper portion of this length was more polluted than in any other part of the river; there was also deep deposit of sewerage matter upon the sloping banks exposed at low tide."[45]

Charles Eliot, the landscape architect, developed a plan to transform the Charles River basin. It called for the construction of a dam near the mouth of the river on the site of the present Science Museum that would wholly exclude the tides, and the gradual development of the entire tidal basin as a recreational facility.[46] The city needed parkland, the Metropolitan District Commission noted in 1895, and "nowhere west of the State House can so much well-distributed space be had for so little money as on the banks of the Charles River."

Eliot's plan did not find easy acceptance among the coal, wood, and lumber dealers of Brighton who feared business ruin in consequence of the project.[47] The opposition succeeded in delaying the project for more than a decade; in 1907, however, the Charles River Dam was at length constructed, and the tidal river passed into history.

95

Even before the construction of the dam, the area of the river between North Harvard and Market Streets was being improved behind dikes. Here a one-mile long race course, the Charles River Speedway, opened in 1899. The sport of harness racing was very popular at the time.[48]

In the 1890s Harvard University purchased eighty acres in Allston from the heirs of Emery Willard, a local coal dealer and farmer.[49] The college built an athletics facility, Carey Cage, and a playing field on the property in 1897. Harvard Stadium replaced the playing field in 1903. This giant structure of reinforced concrete which seats 55,000 spectators was the first permanent large-scale arena for American college athletics.[50] The Harvard Business School, consisting of the monumental Baker Library, classroom, dormitory, and office structures, was built on the opposite side of North Harvard Street in 1927. The neo-classical complex was designed by McKim, Mead, and White.[51]

In the period of 1880 to 1912 several Roman Catholic institutions took over Brighton estates that would otherwise have been subdivided for development. In March of 1880 Father Patrick J. Rogers, the first resident Pastor of St. Columbkille's Parish, purchased the 40-acre Stanwood estate on Foster Street as a site for a Catholic cemetery. Archbishop John Williams had meanwhile been looking for a sizeable parcel of land for the establishment of a seminary for the training of Boston priests. When he heard about Father Rogers' purchase, the Archbishop is reputed to have said: "Not a cemetery, father, a Seminary!"[52]

According to a history of St. John's Seminary, the estate, which was "situated on the east side of Lake Street on wooded land rising above the ponds which gave the street its name . . . combined natural beauty and sufficient seclusion from the city with a comfortable accessibility." Work on the Norman chateau-style building, which was constructed of darkish Brighton puddingstone quarried on

96

the grounds, was begun in 1881. Three years were required to complete the east wing and chapel, which together cost $150,000.[53]

The establishment in 1890 of St. Joseph's Academy, a girl's school, marked the coming to Brighton of the second of these Roman Catholic institutions. The academy, which opened in 1891, occupied the former Henry B. Goodenough estate on Cambridge Street.[54]

Allston-Brighton's Catholic institutions proliferated in the early 1900s. A Catholic hospital for the terminally ill, St. John of God, opened on Allston Street in 1908.[55]

St. Gabriel's Monastery, a retreat house and church operated by the Passionist Religious Society, was also established in 1908. William Cardinal O'Connell noted in a 1927 address dedicating the present St. Gabriel's Church: "I chose, almost by accident, the site of St. Gabriel's Monastery. I happened to be passing by, turned in here and found on the grounds a rather shattered old mansion which had once been a beautiful residence. The proprietors had died, or moved away. As I looked around [on] one of the most beautiful panoramas I had ever seen . . . the thought flashed to my mind that it would be wonderful . . . for a religious house dedicated to retreats for Catholic Laymen."[56]

The Monastery building, which dates from 1909, was designed by T. Edward Sheehan and is the best example of Spanish Mission-style architecture in Boston. The grounds were laid out by the landscaping firm of Frederick Law Olmsted, designer of New York's Central Park. The chapel, which the Passionist Missionary Society established in a converted Nevins estate barn, was replaced in 1927 by St. Gabriel's Church, the work of Maginnis and Walsh, leading ecclesiastical architects of the day.[57]

Cenacle Convent also came to Brighton in this era. In 1911 the Religious of the Cenacle located on a 17-acre site

97

at the eastern end of Nonantum Hill facing Lake Street. They operated at first out of an old farmhouse on the crest of the hill, the Solomon Poor House. The present modern Gothic convent, designed by Maginnis and Walsh, was constructed in stages, beginning in 1922.[58]

The Catholic institution that has had the greatest material impact on Allston-Brighton, St. Elizabeth's Hospital, moved from the South End in 1914, establishing itself on eight acres of the old Nevins property facing Cambridge Street.[59] The original Spanish Mission-style hospital building was designed by Edward F. Graham.

As the number of Roman Catholics in Brighton increased, three additional churches of that denomination were established: the beautiful Romanesque revival St. Anthony's in North Allston in 1894; Our Lady of the Presentation in Oak Square in 1908; and St. Gabriel's in 1909. The Our Lady's congregation at first met in a garage on Faneuil Street. The present Gothic-style church was built in stages between 1913 and 1921.[60]

Other religious denominations established churches in this period as well. Allston's Congregationalists built a magnificent shingle and stone structure on Quint Avenue in 1893, the work of native architect Eugene Clark.[61] The Unitarian First Church moved to a new Gothic structure on Chestnut Hill Avenue in 1895.[62] In the same year Allston's Episcopalians founded St. Lukes Church on Brighton Avenue. They built the present brick Jacobethan-style edifice next to the original wooden structure in 1913.[63] North Allston's Baptists opened the Hill Memorial Baptist Church on North Harvard Street in 1903. The Oak Square Methodist Church was founded in 1911. The Congregationalists of the Faneuil section built a church at the corner of Brooks and Bigelow Streets in 1913. A new Brighton Congregational Church was constructed in 1921 following the destruction of the old building by fire.[64]

Allston-Brighton changed fundamentally in these years. By 1910 a first-rate transportation system, pleasant surroundings, and adequate public services had combined to create a predominantly upper-middle-class neighborhood. With a population of 27,000, Allston-Brighton had, in fact, attained its optimal level of development.

CHAPTER VIII

The Yankee Exodus
1910–1930

In 1910 Allston-Brighton stood on the threshold of a second period of rapid development. Over the next twenty years its population would again double, rising from 27,000 to 60,000, becoming the most densely populated of Boston's outer neighborhoods.[1] A major ethnic transformation also occurred. In 1910 the number of Yankees slightly exceeded the Irish. In 1909, for example, four of the five electoral positions filled by local voters were held by Yankees.[2] Over the next twenty years, however, large numbers of Yankees moved out of Allston-Brighton, while a sizeable number of middle-class Irish and smaller numbers of middle-class Jews and immigrant Italians moved in.

Superficially, Allston-Brighton seemed well prepared to meet the challenge of rapid growth. Many fraternal, ethnic, religious, educational, athletic, civic, and neighborhood organizations had sprung into existence since the 1890s. But it would be a mistake to confuse this activity with strength; the community was, in fact, deeply divided along ethnic lines. The history of the local women's club movement illustrates the social segregation of the period.

Women's clubs were being organized throughout the United States in these years. The movement's central organization, the General Federation of Women's Clubs, could claim a million or more members in 1920. In these clubs, notes one historian, "middle-aged, middle-class women whose children were in school, whose homes were cleaned by servants and supplied commercially with all manner of goods and services, found . . . an antidote to boredom."[3] The local movement was launched in 1896 when a group of Yankee women founded the Brighthelmstone Club. Over the next quarter century this organization established an impressive record of service to Allston-Brighton, particularly in the fields of public health and public education. Despite a major shift in the ethnic composition of the community, the Brighthelmstone Club was as thoroughly Yankee in 1923 as it had been in 1896.[4] While the club did not specifically exclude Irish women, neither did it seek them out. Overt exclusion was unnecessary. Ethnicity was a fundamental aspect of life in Boston in this period. Rose Fitzgerald Kennedy described Boston's social segregation in her autobiography *Times to Remember*. "Separate society columns were published in the newspapers," she wrote, "one about them, one about us."[5] It is thus hardly surprising to find Allston-Brighton's Irish women establishing their own organization, the Brighton Women's Club, in 1924.[6]

A similar pattern of social segregation emerges in the activities of the community's improvement associations. The Faneuil Improvement Association (FIA) was the most active neighborhood-based civic group in Allston-Brighton in the 1910 to 1930 period. The organization had been established in 1895 "to promote the welfare of the western section of Allston-Brighton."[7] Like the Brighthelmstone Club, its membership was solidly Yankee. As late as 1919, 85 percent of its general membership and all but one of its officers was a Yankee.[8] The FIA's experiences furnish a key example of the growing disillusionment with the City of Boston and the future prospects of Allston-Brighton that fueled the Yankee exodus of the 1910 to 1930 period.

The western section of Allston-Brighton had many natural advantages. A good transportation system, both by streetcar and rail, linked the neighborhood to downtown Boston. By 1910 many handsome large-scale residences had already been built along its streets and the potential for continued upper middle-class development seemed promising. About two-thirds of its residents were Yankees.[9]

The FIA had a very specific set of objectives for their section including "properly constructed and maintained streets; sidewalks and public grounds; ample school accommodations; safe hygienic arrangements; a good water supply; fire and police protection; rapid, safe and cheap transit; protect[ion] of natural scenery; and [the use of] all legitimate means to beautify and make attractive both public and private property in this section of the city."[10]

The FIA's most important objective, however, was the widening of Faneuil Street, the neighborhood's main thoroughfare. "There has not within the past fifteen years been an improvement of greater moment, or that means more to the future of Brighton and Faneuil," the secretary of the FIA asserted in 1911.[11] Though the project would require the expenditure of an estimated $235,000, its proponents argued that the cost would be offset by "what the city would gain in taxes by the development of hundreds and hundreds of acres of land abutting on the north and south sides of Faneuil Street, and on adjoining streets, nearly all of which is taxed as farmland, but which would be made available for residential purposes."[12]

Two events of the years 1909 and 1910 profoundly changed Boston's political landscape. A major charter reform backed by the Good Government Association and the Boston Chamber of Commerce strengthened the power of the Mayor by lengthening his term from two to four years and by giving him an absolute veto over all acts

102

of the City Council. As the *Boston Globe* put it, the 1909 reform turned the Mayor of Boston into a "Municipal Monarch."[13] In addition, it abolished the city's bicameral legislative branch which had consisted of a thirteen-member Board of Aldermen and a Common Council. The latter body had included three representatives from each of the city's twenty-five wards. A single nine-member City Council elected on an at-large basis was substituted. Allston-Brighton was thus deprived of direct representation in city government, a situation that would prevail until 1925.[14] Local voters supported these changes in the charter referendum by a 55 to 45 percent margin.[15]

The city's reform forces were prepared to see the powers of the Mayor of Boston expanded because they believed that Boston's next chief executive, to be elected in January 1910, would be James Jackson Storrow, a Yankee financier and reformer. Another feature of their reform package, the institution of non-partisan elections, was calculated to weaken the position of his principal opponent, former Mayor and Democratic ward boss John F. "Honey Fitz" Fitzgerald.[16] But the result was not to be as the reformers had envisioned. Characterizing his contest with Storrow as a struggle of "the people against the money interest," Fitzgerald succeeded in winning a narrow victory over his Yankee opponent.[17] The 1910 election marked the beginning of Irish political domination of Boston. In the next decade Mayor Fitzgerald and his successor, James Michael Curley, built an extensive patronage network in the city's police, fire, public works, and school departments.[18] Irish votes controlled the vast majority of elective offices and Irish neighborhoods received the most benefits and services.

Although the Faneuil Improvement Association's by-laws did not allow it to endorse candidates, there can be little question that the association identified with Storrow's candidacy. They shared his reform philosophy.

103

All the 1909 public meetings of the FIA featured reform speakers. The organization's April 1909 gathering, for example, heard Lincoln Steffens on "Civic Improvement and How To Get It."[19] When a James J. Storrow Club of Ward 25 was organized at the outset of the campaign, several FIA leaders accepted appointment to its Board of Directors.[20] John H. Knowles, a former three-term president of the FIA, held a reception for Storrow when the candidate canvassed the ward in December 1909.[21] And finally there was the verdict of the local electorate. Storrow defeated Fitzgerald in the Faneuil section by a decisive 58 to 39 percent margin.[22]

The politics of the FIA and the Faneuil section did not help its relationship with the Fitzgerald administration. When the new Mayor visited Allston-Brighton in February 1910 to hear requests for public improvements, eight representatives of the FIA presented him with a lengthy list that included major street construction (particularly the widening of Faneuil Street), a new grammar school, a firehouse and library reading room, a bathouse on the Charles River, and more efficient street cleaning and ash and garbage removal.[23]

The Fitzgerald administration, which built schools, playgrounds, and streets on an unprecedented scale between 1910 and 1913, made only one major capital improvement in the Faneuil section: the building of the Oak Square Fire Station in 1913.[24] In the 1914 mayoral race the voters of Faneuil found themselves once again on the losing side when James Michael Curley narrowly defeated South Boston political boss, Thomas Kenny.[25] To an even greater extent than his predecessor, Curley concentrated the city's resources in friendly neighborhoods like the South End, Roxbury, South Boston, and Charlestown. Yankee sections of the city received scant attention; even basic services were withheld. Such practices served to widen the breach between the Yankees and Irish.[26] In Curley's first

104

Washington Street east of Oak Square about 1915.

term, from 1914 to 1917, only one major public facility was constructed in the Faneuil section, the six-room Mary Lyons School, a structure that was overcrowded from the day it opened its doors in September 1914.[27] Large-scale projects such as the widening of Faneuil Street were consistently vetoed on the grounds of economy.[28]

Some sense of the condition of the streets and sewerage system of Faneuil after a decade of such neglect can be gained from a petition that the Faneuil Men's Club sent to the FIA in May 1919, asking the association to call the City's attention to the sorry condition of Brooks Street, "the main artery of travel" in the Faneuil section. "It is necessary for all pedestrians to wade through mud, water, slush and over dangerous, uneven ground caused by washouts in some places, standing water in many others, which accompany each and every fall of rain or thaw of snow and ice," a situation evidencing, "apparent indifference and evident neglect" on the part of the City.[29]

The Faneuil section was not developing along the lines that the FIA's founders had envisioned. The City's failure to widen Faneuil Street had slowed the development of adjacent acreage. As late as 1925 large parcels of adjoining land were still totally undeveloped.[30] Moreover, the scale of the housing being built in the neighborhood in the 1910 to 1930 period changed as the non-Yankee population increased. Prior to 1910 virtually all the houses in the area had been of the spacious, single-family variety. After 1910, however, smaller singles and two and three-family dwellings predominated. The construction of three-deckers particularly displeased the FIA. In a 1919 petition to Mayor Andrew J. Peters, the association noted that "the Faneuil section is the only large area of [Allston-Brighton] having large tracts available for residential building. It is a fact that three-deckers . . . have discouraged the erection of the single and two-family type of home . . . . We believe that immediate steps should be taken to prevent this fire hazard and detriment to the best interest of the community."[31]

As the prospects for upper middle-class development diminished, so did the vitality and morale of the Faneuil Improvement Association. By 1916 the association was meeting less often, its elaborate committee structure was breaking down, and its aspirations for the neighborhood were less ambitious. Faneuil's Yankee residents were losing confidence in the future prospects of the neighborhood. Yet no effort was made to adjust to the new political realities. No attempt was made to enhance the Association's influence by sharing its leadership with the Irish. The FIA continued solidly Yankee in ethos to the last. When Boston's largely Irish police force struck for higher wages in 1919, thirty-one members of the Faneuil Improvement Association signed up to serve as Special Officers, a measure hardly calculated to endear the FIA to Allston-Brighton's growing Irish population.[32] The organization continued to meet intermittently over the next several years, but with less and less energy. The FIA finally expired in the late 1920s.

The 1910 to 1930 period saw the Faneuil section transformed from a majority Yankee to a majority Irish neighborhood. In 1910 the Yankees held two-thirds of the property in Faneuil; by 1930 the Irish owned more than half of the homes in the neighborhood.[33] In 1910 a clear majority of Faneuil's residents had been members of the upper middle class—professional men, business executives, and the like; by 1930, middle-class Irish, many holding secure municipal jobs, were in the majority.[34] The shift in Faneuil's ethnic composition led to a dramatic increase in the membership of the local Catholic church, Our Lady of the Presentation.[35] In 1910, 55 percent of affiliated voters had been Republicans; the comparable figure for 1930 was 33 percent.[36] The Yankee exodus even extended to the leaders of the FIA. About half of early members of the association had moved out of Allston-Brighton by 1930, most of them relocating in more affluent and politically compatible suburbs like Brookline, Newton, and Wellesley.[37]

The Yankee exodus was but one element in complex major demographic changes that occurred between 1910 and 1930. At least equally significant was the rise of the Commonwealth Avenue section. Though the avenue itself dated from the 1890s, the surrounding acreage experienced remarkable little development until 1910, when a major building boom began. In the 1915 to 1920 period, the area registered a 38 percent increase in population, the fastest growth rate in Boston.[38] A combination of handsome architecture and broad vistas made this one of the city's most desirable neighborhoods. In 1919, for example, more high ranking city and county officials resided in Allston-Brighton, chiefly in the Commonwealth Avenue section, than in any other Boston neighborhood, with Jamaica Plain a close second. The list included the City Treasurer, Superintendent of Schools, Secretary of the School Committee, Commissioners of the Building Department; also, the President of the Board of Trustees of the Boston Public Library and the Clerks of the Municipal and the Superior Courts.[39]

With the development of the Commonwealth Avenue section also began the first major influx of Jews into Allston-Brighton. A small community of mostly immigrant Jews had existed in North Brighton as early as the 1890s, probably attracted to that locality by the kosher meat businesses at the Brighton Abattoir. The Jews who moved into the Commonwealth Avenue section in the 1910 to 1930 period, however, were not immigrants, but their affluent, often well-educated sons and daughters. Jewish investors played a major part in the development of the area; in 1925 they owned about half the buildings on Commonwealth Avenue.[40] In March 1917 members of the recently organized Congregation Kehillath Isreal met in the home of Bernard Steuer on Chester Street, Allston to plan the construction of the temple that now stands at 384 Harvard Street in Brookline.[41] The number of Jews in the Commonwealth Avenue area increased rapidly. By 1920 there were seven kosher meat markets in the Commonwealth Avenue section. The number had doubled by 1930.[42]

The first Jewish religious congregation in Allston-Brighton, Aharath Achim, was established in North Brighton in 1928. It met in a house on Lawrence Place, adjacent to the Portsmouth Street Playground until 1940, when it unaccountably expired.[43] The most important local congregation, B'nai Moshe, was founded by the Jews of the Commonwealth Avenue section in 1932. A store on Chestnut Hill Avenue served as its first headquarters. In 1933 the members purchased a private residence at the southeast corner of Chestnut Hill Avenue and Wallingford Road for conversion to a temple.[44] In the following year they acquired a distinquished scholar, Joseph Shalom Shubow, as their rabbi.[45]

By 1930 Allston-Brighton's Jewish population stood at about 5,000, or approximately 15 percent of the total population of the Commonwealth Avenue section. The first Jewish resident to win public office was Jennie Loitman Barron, who was elected to an at-large seat on the Boston School Committee in 1925. An educational reformer and women's rights advocate, Barron was later appointed to the Massachusetts Superior Court, the first woman to serve on that tribunal.[46]

The rise of the Commonwealth Avenue section gave new vitality to a sagging Republican Party. In the 1901 to 1909 period the Republicans had dominated local races, winning 35 out of 44 Allston-Brighton contests for the State Legislature and Common Council.[47] Party registration was virtually even by 1910: 1783 Republicans, 1751 Democrats and 1306 Independents.[48] The Yankee exodus further weakened the Republican Party. Had it not been for the rise of the affluent and heavily Republican Commonwealth Avenue section, Allston-Brighton might have become a Democratic bastion at an earlier date in its history. As it was, the parties occupied a position of approximately equal strength for some years longer. Political competitiveness was reduced, however, in 1916 when Allston-Brighton became two wards. The South Allston and Commonwealth Avenue sections retained the designation Ward 25, while North Allston and the western part of the district became Ward 26.[49] Throughout the 1916 and 1930 period, Ward 25 elected Republicans and Ward 26 elected Democrats with regularity.

The settlement of large numbers of Italians in Allston-Brighton after 1910 added another key ethnic element to the community. In contrast to the Jews, most of the Italians were poor immigrants. They often arrived without families, so-called "birds of passage," seasonal laborers who came to earn enough money, return to the homeland, and buy a plot of land. But the inducements to permanent settlement were powerful.

Italians sought the comfort and security of the immigrant enclave. They settled in the two oldest sections of the community, the Winship-Shepard-Shannon Street area, just east of Brighton Center, and North Brighton. They were drawn to these locations initially by cheap housing and later by the presence of settlers from their own town or region of Italy. More than half those living in the Winship-Shepard-Shannon Street area in 1930, for example, came from the same village in south central Italy, San Donato Val di Comino.[50]

By 1926 the local Italian community was large enough to warrant the selection of Allston-Brighton as the site for the Massachusetts Sons of Italy State Convention. The agenda of the convention included a parade through the streets of Brighton, a stop at the newly dedicated Benedetto Viola Square where services were held honoring the World War I veterans, and a gathering of the delegates in Brighton Center's Warren Hall. By 1930 the Italian population of Allston-Brighton stood at about 3,500.[51]

Immigrants from other nations also settled in Allston-Brighton in this period, including Lithuanians, Jews, Poles, Armenians, Greeks, Syrians. The Franklin Street area of North Allston attracted a small concentration of Near Eastern immigrants. By 1925 the North Bennett

110

Street Community Center, an immigrant social service agency with a headquarters on Lincoln Street in North Brighton, was serving an estimated 1000 immigrants a month, representing eight nationalities. The center provided its clients with English and civic classes, assistance in completing citizenship applications, a library, and a baby clinic.[52]

Allston-Brighton had to be concerned with more than its own growing pains in this period; national and international events also influenced the life of the community. When the United States entered World War I on April 6, 1917, President Woodrow Wilson declared, "It is not an army that we must shape and train for war, it is a nation."[53] The Allston-Brighton community responded to that challenge with great fervor. As early as April 9, 1917, local residents flocked to the Allston Theatre on Brighton Avenue for a Patriotic Demonstration.[54] Volunteers rushed to fill the ranks of the local Home Guard Company, which had the responsibility of protecting railroads, factories, and other key installations.[55] Women's groups were especially active in war work. The Brighton-Allston branch of the American Red Cross, the Special Aid Society, the St. Columbkille's Parish Preparedness Unit, and other organizations produced clothing for soldiers at the front, surgical dressings, convalescent gowns, pajamas, and shirts for the medical service; sponsored talks on food production, canning, and preservation; promoted the sale of War Bonds; and engaged in a wide variety of war-related fundraising projects.[56] Hundreds of local acres were converted into "Victory Gardens." The students at St. John's, for example, planted twelve acres of the Seminary grounds with potatoes, corn, beets, turnips, carrots, tomatoes, and cabbages.[57]

It was not until September 1917 that Allston-Brighton dispatched its first quota of draftees to Camp Devens. An estimated five thousand flag-waving residents rallied in

111

front of the District 14 Police Station to give the seventy-one men a "royal send off."[58] In the months that followed, "Letters from the Front" became a regular feature of the *Item's* front page. With the appearance of the first casualty notices in the spring of 1918 anti-German feelings intensified.

When word of victory reached Allston-Brighton in November 1918, the *Item* marked the event with the front page publication of a verse by Longfellow:

> Peace! and no longer from its brazen portals
> The blast of war's great organ shakes the skies!
> But beautiful as songs of the immortals,
> The holy melodies of love arise.[59]

The general public was less restrained and less loving in its response, however:

> Mrs. Thomas Still, who has a son in the service—with a dishpan camouflaged as a drum, paraded through the streets. She was soon joined by other residents . . . leading a hilarious band of youngsters who aided in making a merry din . . . . The boys, right on hand when there is any celebrating to be done, formed a street parade and Kaiser Bill bearing a dagger in his straw heart was borne through Brooks street to the Arsenal where a guard was invited to do a little bayonet practice."[60]

An enormous amount of building occurred in Allston-Brighton in the post-World-War-I era. Note has already been taken of the number of Catholic institutions that located in the district in the 1880 to 1915 period: St. John's Seminary (1881), Mount St. Joseph's Academy (1886), the St. John of God Hospital (1908), St. Gabriel's Monastery (1909), the Cenacle Convent (1911), St. Elizabeth's

112

Hospital (1912), the latter a well established inner city institution which moved from the congested South End to enlarged quarters in suburban Brighton.[61] William Cardinal O'Connell contributed significantly to the expansion of these facilities. In 1918 theater owner Benjamin F. Keith bequeathed the Archdiocese more than $2 million. The Cardinal, who loved beautiful architecture, used the money to create a "Little Rome" on the hills of Brighton. One of the buildings he constructed with the Keith money was the Archbishop's residence on Commonwealth Avenue, an Italian Renaissance palace, dating from 1926.[62]

As Allston-Brighton's population increased, so did the need for public facilities. The 1923 to 1930 period, in fact, witnessed an unprecedented expansion of school facilities. School buildings constructed in this eight-year period included the Andrew Jackson (1923), the Alexander Hamilton (1924), the James A. Garfield (1925), the Harriet Baldwin (1927), and after years of community agitation, a new Brighton High School in 1930. A new municipal courthouse, another major project of the period, was completed in 1927.[63]

The two decades that ended in 1930 had been years of unparalleled physical expansion for Allston-Brighton. As the decade of the twenties drew to a close, few imagined that the nation was about to be plunged into the greatest economic crisis of its history.

CHAPTER IX

The Great Depression—World War II Post-War Development

1930–1960

The half century that ended in 1930 had witnessed a ten-fold increase in Allston-Brighton's population. This incredible rate of development began levelling off in the twenties as the supply of land diminished. It slowed to an even greater extent in the depression years of the thirties. In the post-World-War-II era, however, a second period of intense development saw the population of Allston-Brighton rise to an all-time high of 73,000.[1]

Before proceeding to describe Allston-Brighton during the depression, note should be taken of the construction of two rather important landmarks.

The first, the Egyptian Theater, was built in 1929. Prior to its opening, motion pictures had been shown at Billy Woods, or the Barn, on Market Street to the rear of the Washington Building and at Odd Fellow's Hall in Allston. With the introduction of talkies in 1927, audiences expanded to such an extent that larger theaters were required. With a seating capacity of 1,700, the Egyptian was one of the handsomest of these movie palaces.[2] Two other large motion picture theaters existed in Allston-Brighton: the Capital Theater on Commonwealth Avenue and the converted Allston Theater on the south side of Brighton Avenue, just east of the Harvard Avenue intersection; the latter had been built in 1912 for stage productions.[3] On the eighth anniversary of the opening of the

Interior of the Egyptian Theater, Brighton Center.

Egyptian Theater the *Item* took the measure of the impact of sound movies by noting: "The miracle of talkies has entered into the everyday life and existence of the Brighton section and has brightened endless hours with music, song, romance and comedy such as no other visible medium might create."[4]

On October 2, 1930 the present Brighton High School on Warren Street was dedicated at a public banquet, the first event in a four-day celebration of Boston's 300th anniversary.[5] Possibly Boston's finest example of modern Gothic architecture, the U-shaped structure was specially adapted to a lot that sloped more than 40 feet from front to rear and that was divided by an outcropping of ledge. It was designed by the architectural firm of O'Connell and Shaw.[6]

Then, of course, in the fall of 1929 the stockmarket crashed and the decade of economic distress known as the Great Depression settled upon the nation. Allston-Brighton suffered its share of hardships in the depression. Trade fell off in local stores and businesses failed, particularly those dealing in luxury commodities such as automobiles. Allston was then Boston's automotive center. Brighton Avenue, Commonwealth Avenue, and North Beacon Street were lined with auto dealerships, agencies, and accessory supply houses. On the eve of the depression the area contained 117 automobile-related business establishments. This industry contracted by more than one third in the first four years of depression.[7]

The condition of the local construction industry provides another measure of the depression's impact on Allston-Brighton. Houses were still being built in fairly impressive numbers in the 1930 to 1934 period—some 50 a year. Prior to the economic crisis, however, the rate had been much higher, nearly 200 a year.[8] This decline in construction represented a serious hardship for the large number of contractors, artisans, and laborers who lived in Allston-Brighton. However, the fact that any construction was going on in a period when 10 million Americans were unemployed and businesses were collapsing left and right suggests that Allston-Brighton was relatively well off in the depression years.[9]

A city administration under James Michael Curley provided a small measure of relief by spending heavily on public works projects and public assistance in the years prior to the establishment of the Works Progress Administration by the New Deal. A library and two schools were constructed in the 1931–1933 period—the Faneuil Library, dating from 1931, and the Thomas A. Edison Junior High and Barrett Elementary School, dating from 1932 and 1933 respectively.[10]

Significantly, the population of Allston-Brighton continued to increase in the depression years, rising by an impressive 16 percent between 1930 and 1935.[11] This growth in population evidences the desirability of the Allston-Brighton neighborhood in that era of general distress.

The appearance of a second weekly, the *Citizen*, in 1935 attests to the relative economic health of Allston-Brighton in the depression era. Its publisher, G. Russell Phinney, bought out the *Item* in 1947. The combined paper was called the *Citizen* until 1960. For a time separate Allston and Brighton editions were published, but with little variation of content. It appeared as the *Citizen-Item* from 1960 to 1984, then reverted to its original name, the *Item*.[12]

The year 1937 witnessed the construction of another depression era project, the Leo Birmingham Parkway, named for a recently deceased state legislator.[13] The city had two objectives in building the Parkway: a reduction of traffic congestion at the bottom of Market Street and an extension of the green space on the margin of the Charles River around the sprawling abattoir complex. Some urged the city to wait until the outmoded abattoir closed, raze the facility, and extend Soldiers' Field Road directly through the site, developing the surrounding land for recreational use; but this sensible proposal was ignored.[14] When the Brighton Abattoir finally closed its doors in the 1950s, it was succeeded by a nondescript commercial complex, the greatest eyesore on the Charles River between Boston and Watertown. The construction of the Soldiers' Field Road Extension diverted traffic from the parkway, leaving it one of the most under-utilized roads in Allston-Brighton.

The city created two additional Allston-Brighton parks in the early 1940s. A proposal had been advanced to purchase Chandler's Pond for parkland as early as 1927. This scenic body of water, nestled between Nonantum and Waban Hills, was in real danger of obliteration by

117

developers. A portion had already been filled to create Lake Shore Road and two-family houses were being constructed on the Kenrick Street side. The city refused to purchase the property, arguing that "its proximity to Rogers Park, one of the largest parks in the city," gave it little utility; that the money should instead be spent on improving existing parks. Fortunately, wiser counsels prevailed. The pond was purchased, and in 1941, during the administration of Maurice Tobin, the Alice Gallagher Park was established on its south margin.[15]

The second addition to the local park system was made in August 1941 when City Councillor Maurice Sullivan persuaded the Boston Elevated, which owned a parcel of land of the east side of Oak Square, to lease a portion of the property to the city for a dollar a year for the creation of the Oak Square Playground.[16]

1941 also saw the conversion of the old fire station on Chestnut Hill Avenue, gutted by fire in 1939, into a municipal building. The community had been agitating for such a facility for more than thirty years.[17]

The outbreak of war in Europe in 1939 had little impact on Allston-Brighton. The Japanese attack on Pearl Harbor on December 7, 1941, however, was another matter. There was widespread fear that eastern cities like Boston would be bombed. The Watertown Arsenal, a major munitions facility, provided the enemy with a local target. As early as December 9, two days after Pearl Harbor, Allston-Brighton held its first air raid drill. Residents were instructed to clear their attics of combustible material, to keep their bath tubs and other receptacles filled with water in case of incendiary bombing, to put in a supply of sand to extinguish fires, and to build bomb shelters in their cellars.[18]

The army took immediate steps to protect Allston-Brighton from air raids. Anti-aircraft guns were placed at five locations: the intersection of Brooks and North

118

Beacon Streets; on Wexford Avenue (a discontinued street adjacent to the Birmingham Parkway); on Perthshire Road at the top of Bigelow Hill; at the Harvard Stadium; and, finally, behind the Commonwealth Armory. The proximity of four of these installations to the Watertown Arsenal should be noted.[19]

When President Roosevelt delivered his war message to Congress at 10 p.m. on Tuesday, December 9, the entire country stopped to listen. A minstrel show at the Brighton Avenue Baptist Church was interrupted and a radio carried to the stage so that no one would miss the historic address.[20]

World War II influenced the life of Allston-Brighton in the same ways it was influencing life in thousands of communities across the United States. There were air raid drills and blackouts; wartime shortages necessitated rationing; lists of inductees appeared each week in the local press; women's, church, and civic organizations took up war-related projects (community fund campaigns for the U.S.O., Red Cross classes, and the like); war movies such as "Devil Dogs of the Air" and "West Point Widow," the Egyptian's offerings on August 16, 1942, were popular fare; and, of course, with increasing frequence from 1943 onward, casualty notices began appearing.

A major housing shortage existed in the post-war years. Few new units had been built during the depression, when money was in short supply, or during the war, when building material was scarce. The government met the housing need, particularly critical in the case of returning war veterans, by building many large-scale housing developments. Two were constructed locally—the Faneuil and Fidelis Way projects. The 258-unit Faneuil housing development reached completion in 1950.[21]

The Fidelis Way project was built on the site of Brighton's last farm, operated by the Middlemas brothers. In the mid-1930s a private developer had proposed constructing 1700 units on this property, which commanded a spectacular view of the city; but the economy of the depression era had not been favorable.[22] The Middlemas farm was prime real estate. The manner of its development —its design, style, density, and elevation—were matters that would have an important long-range impact on the community. Construction of the 648-unit project began in October 1949 and reached completion in May 1951.[23]

The most active neighborhood association of the 1950s, the Aberdeen Civic and Improvement Association, arose in response to a zoning change that would have allowed the construction of a third major veteran's housing project on a large city-owned parcel of land between Chestnut Hill Avenue and Wallingford Road. Arguing that the proposed project was totally unsuited to the character and scale of the surrounding neighborhood and would place an insupportable burden on local schools and streets, the association obtained a Superior Court order barring construction.[24] "Without the very determined opposition of the Aberdeen Association," the *Citizen* noted, "a project would have been put up in a section quite unsuited to it." As would frequently be the case, however, development was merely deferred. Twenty years later a large-scale elderly housing development arose on this site.[25]

Brighton and Allston faced a succession of such critical land-use issues in the post-war years. With a population of 70,000 occupying just four square miles, it had the highest density level of any of the city's outer suburbs. In 1946 a Boston Planning Board survey of land available for development in the city's neighborhoods showed Allston-Brighton with the smallest amount. Dorchester had 155 acres; Hyde Park, 310; West Roxbury, 824. Allston-Brighton's total was a meager 16½ acres.[26]

Moreover, the community suffered from two basic handicaps in attempting to control indiscriminate development: (1) Widespread public indifference: while

120

proposals sometimes generated opposition among those directly influenced, the general population was disposed to welcome development; and, (2) political powerlessness. Boston is governed under a strong Mayor City Charter. Containing less than 10 percent of Boston's voters and holding just two seats on the relatively powerless 22 member city council, Allston-Brighton was not in a position to exercise effective control over the development process, even had it been of a mind to do so.

Then, in 1949, an already bad political situation grew worse when the city's reform forces pushed through a charter change providing that from 1951 Councillors would be elected not from individual districts, but on an at-large basis. From the standpoint of basic constituent services, the 22-member district council had served the community well. If a district councillor failed to satisfy constituent needs, there was a good chance that he would be replaced in the next election; not so the at-large council. Its broad electoral base insulated it against the dissatisfaction of any one neighborhood. Also, there was no assurance under this system that all of the city's neighborhoods would be represented. The Allston-Brighton community fared well in the first few elections under the new charter; but with the retirement of Francis X. Ahearn from the City Council in 1957, Brighton and Allston ceased to be represented in city government. For the next quarter century, a community of nearly 70,000 people, the second largest neighborhood in Boston, was without a voice in city hall.[27]

In addition to the Fidelis Way and Faneuil Projects, the early 1950s saw the construction of several hundred units of housing on Washington, Brook, and Fairbanks Streets. Later in the decade, single family homes went up on the land formerly occupied by the Eliot Nurseries on Kenrick Street. Had this land come onto the market in the Sixties, judging from the fate of the adjacent Chestnut Hill

Country Club, apartment buildings would probably occupy the site today.

A major local landmark, The Brighton Abattoir, disappeared in 1956. Few regretted the loss, however. In announcing the sale of the 42-acre riverfront complex to a Boston developer, the *Citizen* described the Abattoir as an "institution which many residents of this vicinity have wished was far away ever since it was established 85 years ago."[28] Rev. Charles N. Cunningham of St. John's Seminary, reflecting on his boyhood in North Brighton in the 1870s, remembered how a beautiful neighborhood of "narrow lanes bordered by butternut trees, thriving nurseries and well-tilled farms disappeared at the coming of the Abattoir" and how "the old settlers moved naturally farther up the hill to other parts of Brighton."[29] The strong odors from the Abattoir's rendering plant had impeded development and depressed property values in the northern section of Brighton for nearly a century. In addition, the industry had been in decline for many years. "This is a once-in-a-lifetime opportunity," the *Citizen* declared, "to get rid of a blighted area that is now occupied by dilapidated buildings and over-run with vermin."[30]

Note has already been taken of the planning implications of the use of this acreage, the only waterfront property between the Charles River Dam and Newton that was not controlled by the MDC. Allston-Brighton's civic and business leaders strongly favored light industrial and commercial development of the site. Local businesses were hurting in the late 1950s as residents began shifting their patronage from neighborhood stores to suburban shopping centers. It was hoped that the development of the Abattoir acreage would help offset this distressing trend.[31] While the eighteen-building Abattoir complex was promptly demolished, new buildings did not arise until 1960, following the construction of the Soldiers Field Road Extension, and the economic benefits of development of the site fell far short of the high expectations of 1956.[32] Traffic congestion was another major problem in the post-war period. Two local arteries, Brighton Avenue-North Beacon Street and Commonwealth Avenue, were carrying most of the east-west commuter traffic. So many accidents were occurring on Commonwealth Avenue in the late 1940s that the *Citizen* dubbed the roadway "The Boulevard of Broken Limbs." As the paper wrote in 1948:

Something has to be done about Commonwealth Avenue, the broad and landscaped parkway that is perhaps Allston-Brighton's handsomest thoroughfare and undoubtedly its most lethal one. Multi-laned, well-paved, and alluring to the motorist made fretful by the cold molasses in Boston's ever cooking traffic jam, it is the Circe of highways. It's as treacherous and as cruel as a Nazi booby trap.[33]

The problem eased somewhat over the next several years as roadways were expanded and modernized. Local improvements included the elimination of a raised street-car reservation on Brighton Avenue, design changes on Commonwealth Avenue, and the resurfacing of Cambridge, Washington, and North Beacon Streets.[34] But it was the construction of three major thoroughfares— Storrow Drive, a four-lane highway linking North Brighton with North Station, the Soldier's Field Road extension, and the Massachusetts Turnpike Extension— that did the most to relieve the congestion problem.[35]

Parking was an equally serious dilemma. A city ordinance required the nighttime removal of motor vehicles from the streets, but a shortage of offstreet parking and garage space made this an impossibility. Further complicating the situation was a 1937 State Superior Court decision forbidding the use of streets for the nighttime storage of automobiles.[36] In 1952 and 1954, however, the state legislature passed laws authorizing the Boston Traffic Commission to allow all-night parking.[37] Alternate-side parking systems were tried for a time, but proved impractical. Trees were a primary victim of the parking crisis. In 1957 three thousand residents of the Commonwealth Avenue Section signed a petition calling for the removal of 61 trees from Commonwealth Avenue to provide 320 parking spaces. Many Allston-Brighton residents opposed the measure.[38] The Aberdeen Civic and Improvement Association charged that parking spaces on the avenue would lead to "decreased property valuations," and "encroachment of business on [the] area."[39] When the removal of the trees began in October 1957, the *Citizen* noted, "Reaction to the tree chopping has been intense. Allston residents are divided into two camps."[40]

A critical shortage of parking spaces existed in the business areas as well. The Brighton and Allston Boards of Trade pleaded with the city to open municipal parking lots in Brighton Center and in the Harvard Avenue business district. While a small lot was opened in Brighton Center, nothing was done for Allston. "Merchants in Allston are digging deep into their pocket books this week to raise a sum of money . . . to be used in the purchase of a parcel of land at Glenville Avenue for parking facilities," the *Citizen* reported in February 1958.[41]

The Jewish community continued to grow in size and influence in these years as large numbers of Jews left crowded neighborhoods in Roxbury and the West and North Ends to settle in the less congested sections of Boston. By 1950 Jews made up about 20 percent of Allston-Brighton's population and nearly half that of the Commonwealth Avenue section. While Temple B'nai Moshe had outgrown its Chestnut Hill Avenue facility as early as 1940, World War II and the absence of Rabbi Joseph Shubow, who was serving as an army chaplain, delayed construction of a new facility. A handsome new temple and Hebrew School were finally dedicated in December 1949.[42] Jewish political influence increased in this period as well. After 1940 at least one Jew was elected to an Allston-Brighton seat in the State Legislature on a regular basis. Louis Lobel, a Republican attorney, was the first Jew elected to public office by the voters of Allston-Brighton. He served as State Representative from 1941 to 1951.[43] In 1951 a second Jewish congregation, Kadimah-Toras Moshe, established itself at 113 Washington Street, near Commonwealth Avenue.[44] The first building in Boston designed as a Jewish Community Center opened at 50 Sutherland Road in 1956. A Brighton location was chosen not only because of the sizeable local Jewish community but because of the absence of adequate recreational facilities in the crowded Commonwealth Avenue apartment house district.[45]

The post-war era saw still another major Catholic institution locate in Allston-Brighton, the Kennedy Memorial Hospital, which located on Warren Street opposite Brighton High School. Archbishop Richard Cushing broke ground for the new facility on September 17, 1947.[46] The hospital admitted its first patients in September 1949.[47]

Allston-Brighton reached its developmental saturation point in the 1950s. The disposition to see development in purely positive terms gave way to a recognition that further growth would carry a heavy price in the form of lost open space, traffic congestion, noise pollution, and pressure on existing public services. The struggle to confine and channel development, often waged against nearly impossible odds, was to become the central feature of Allston-Brighton's history in the 1960 to 1985 period.

125

CHAPTER X

The Years Since 1960

According to a recent Boston Redevelopment Authority
(BRA) publication, contemporary Allston-Brighton is one
of the "best integrated and most diverse neighborhoods"
in the city—an area in which "high concentrations of
elderly, college students, and working class families
combine to present a wide range of lifestyles." This chapter
will describe some of the forces that helped transform the
still largely "family-oriented" Allston-Brighton of 1960
into the cultural and socio-economic crossroads of our
time.[1]

In 1951 the Boston Planning Board forecast a population
trend that would have particular impact on Allston-
Brighton. "The Planning Board believes," its report read,
"that by 1975 Boston will have fewer young children and
correspondingly fewer adults in the thirty-five to forty-five
age groups; more young adults and more elderly people.
This change in composition will continue the trend
toward smaller family groupings . . . ." By 1980 53.5
percent of Allston-Brighton's residents were young adults
between the ages of 15 and 29, while another 11 percent
were 65 years of age or over; these two groups together
constituted 64.5 percent, or nearly two-thirds of the community's population. The comparable statistic for the city
as a whole was 41.5 percent.[2]

The location of three major universities on the

boundaries of Allston-Brighton helps account for this high young adult population. These schools—Boston University, Boston College, and Harvard University—experienced major growth in the post-World-War-II period.[3] Since their efforts to provide off-campus housing failed to keep pace with increasing enrollments, students sought accommodations in surrounding neighborhoods. In Allston-Brighton, with its relatively permissive zoning regulations, whole neighborhoods were transformed: high rents, subdividion of units, absentee landlordism, physical deterioration, and parking problems were just a few of the by-products of this student influx.

The Planning Board's 1951 prediction of a continuing trend toward smaller family units was likewise borne out locally. Though the number of people in Allston-Brighton is no greater today than it was in 1935, the population is much more in evidence. For one thing, the housing pattern changed radically. Back in 1935 there were just 20,000 units of housing in Allston-Brighton. Families were larger. The elderly typically lived with their children in an extended family arrangement. Today, by contrast, many young adults and elderly residents live on their own. By 1980 the numbers of housing units had risen to 28,000, a figure 40 percent higher than that of 1935.[4]

While the number of residents had remained about the same over the past half century, the number of automobiles on Allston-Brighton's streets has increased by 500 percent. In 1935 there were just 6000 vehicles registered to Allston-Brighton residents. Today motor vehicle registration exceeds 30,000. Thus, much of the congestion the community has experienced in recent years is not so much a product of people or altered housing patterns as it is of this increased number of automobiles and the traffic snarls, parking problems, and noise and air pollution these vehicles generate. In short, the character of Allston-Brighton changed fundamentally in the post-1960 era.

127

The Commonwealth Avenue section, a preferred neighborhood in the twenties and thirties, was particularly hard hit by these developments. By the mid-sixties the *Boston Globe* was describing the Avenue as

> [an] area where once palatial homes have been subdivided into relatively small and sometimes grimy apartments . . . apartments with doors open to all strangers, some with broken mail boxes, trash filled airshafts and noise that breaks easily through the thin walls.

> Here, widows, widowers, pensioners, shut-ins share the same buildings with students from Boston University, Boston College and other schools in the area. It is not a very good recipe for coexistence, but it presumably makes money.

The physical deterioration was not limited to its apartment building zone, the *Globe* noted.

> From the upper middle income neighborhood bordering Newton—to the deteriorating Hanoville district, from the pleasant apartment-lined streets running out of Brookline to the gaudy industrial strips of Allston, the people complain of stolen cars, broken windows, a lack of parks and recreation, schools, break-ins and what they regard as the city's neglect of their community.[5]

Boston's failure to enforce its zoning code contributed significantly to the physical deterioration of Allston-Brighton. In 1967 Joseph M. Smith, President of the Allston Civic Association, accused the Zoning Board of "choking, deteriorating, endangering and destroying the Allston-Brighton community" by "consistently grant[ing] variances allowing landlords to chop up apartments, add to them, turn them into rooming houses and anything else that might be conceived to return a greater profit." Smith described the city's zoning appeals process as a "laughing stock," and called for major changes in the way the agency was appointed.[6]

Requests for zoning variances were of course not limited to the alteration of existing properties, but applied also to new construction. "Building is booming in Brighton—in Allston also according to the latest construction bulletins," the *Citizen-Item* proclaimed in September 1961.[7]

State and city seizure of local properties by eminent domain also generated enormous concern. Commercial property had been taken in the 1950s for the Soldier's Field Road extension, but the first residential landtakings were made in connection with the building of the Massachusetts Turnpike extension through the northern part of Allston-Brighton in 1963 and 1964. In all, eighty families living chiefly on Riverview Road and Lincoln and Vineland Streets were obliged to relocate. Lincoln Street alone lost twenty houses.[8] There was concern for the long-term impact of the construction as well, for, as a BRA publication noted, the Turnpike would have "a more significant negative impact on surrounding neighborhoods than the Penn Central Railroad tracks" owing to the greater amount of "noise and air pollution." It was in response to these concerns that the Allston Civic Association was organized in 1963.[9]

No single issue of the 1960s generated greater controversy than the Boston Redevelopment Authority's seizure for urban renewal of Barry's Corner, a 9.3-acre neighborhood lying at the corner of North Harvard Street and Western Avenue. The struggle between this tiny North Allston neighborhood and the powerful BRA attracted extensive media attention and aroused widespread sympathy. At issue was the right of a governmental agency

129

to demolish older homes to make way for hundreds of units of luxury housing.[10] The BRA claimed that the Barry's Corner neighborhood was "blighted," a charge its residents hotly disputed.

In their campaign to save the neighborhood, the residents left no stone unturned. They organized the Citizens for Private Property which emitted a stream of impassioned press releases. They appealed to every level of government for relief: Boston Mayor John F. Collins, the City Council, the State Planning Board, the General Court, and the Federal Department of Housing, all to no avail. In August 1965 in a last ditch effort to prevent demolition, a delegation from the neighborhood travelled to Washington, D.C. to place their case before the district's Congressional representatives.[11]

While appealing to officialdom for help, the residents declared that they would never peacefully surrender their property. As they viewed the matter, the BRA was stealing their homes. "We are categorically against the acquisition of one man's land for the sake of private profit for another," they declared.[12] "To Hell With Urban Renewal" signs sprouted up in the neighborhood. In the summer of 1964 Barry's Corner showed that it meant to resist:

> A horn blasted throughout the North Harvard Street area Tuesday noon and some thirty citizens turned out in true Minuteman fashion to rout an appraisal team from the Boston Redevelopment Authority.

> Homeowners . . . mustered at Redgate's Store at 162 Harvard Street armed with brooms, shovels, sticks and spades minutes after. Gerald Tetrault and Bernard Redgate drove through the neighborhood sounding the alert.[13]

The appraisal team returned, however, with police support, and by August 1965 most of Barry's Corner had been cleared.[14] Then, with just nine of the original fifty houses remaining, Mayor Collins ordered the suspension of further demolition and appointed a "Blue Ribbon Commission" to reconsider the issue of how best to develop the acreage. This Commission made two recommendations: that the bidding process be reopened and that the deeds of the nine remaining houses be returned to their owners. The Mayor accepted the first suggestion, but rejected the second.[15]

The contract to build on the North Harvard Street Development Area, as the city now called the neighborhood, was ultimately awarded to a local non-profit corporation, the Committee for North Harvard (CNH), whose Board included many Allston-Brighton community leaders. CNH was also cosponsored by five local churches. It proposed to construct 212 units of moderate income housing.[16]

CNH's selection as developer neutralized the Allston-Brighton community which up to that time had been highly supportive of Barry's Corner. The demolition of the remaining structures now moved forward with minimal political damage to the Collins administration.

Final demolition of Barry's Corner occurred in October 1969. In announcing the razing of the remaining structures the *Citizen-Item* noted:

This tragic incident in Brighton must act as a revelation to the weary authorities. The BRA and the city must use this dramatic example of inflexible policies and structured thinking to prevent such a tragedy from recurring. The rending of stable communities cannot possibly benefit anyone in the long run. It can only add to the degradation of human beings at the mercy of their government and take us one step further in the ruination of urban America.[17]

Densely populated Allston-Brighton was lacking in adequate recreational facilities in the post-World-War-II period. The need was partially addressed in the fifties and sixties by the creation of new parks (at Sorrento Street in North Allston, Chiswick Road, and Commonwealth Avenue, and on MDC property on Soldier's Field Road), by the opening of pools on the Charles River and at Cleveland Circle, and the establishment in 1958 of a YMCA at the corner of Lake and Washington Streets.[18] Local recreational facilities were greatly expanded in 1971 when the West End House moved to Allston-Brighton, its former neighborhood having been largely obliterated by urban renewal. According to a recent history of the organization, the Allston-Brighton location was chosen because "it seemed to attract inner-city residents who were intent on moving up the social ladder. It seemed fitting for the West End House, itself led by second and third generation immigrants, to follow the streetcar lines to a community where they could rejoin their clientele." The City of Boston furnished a portion of Ringer Playground for the $1.4 million facility.[19]

The 1960s and 1970s also witnessed a steady encroachment by developers on Allston-Brighton's supply of open land. A former Brighton resident, returning to the Chandler Pond area in 1966 after an absence of twenty-five years, wrote as follows in the *Citizen-Item*:

> Homes have sprouted in the former market garden behind the Edison School and on most of the land west of Brayton Road. Long lines of apartments have replaced the open corrals and rambling barn of Pickens Stable near Chandler's Pond, and an ill-kempt park on filled in land now borders the pond where muskrats lived and wild Iris bloomed.[20]

The "lines of apartments" referred to Towne Estates,

several hundred units of garden apartments which stretch like a Wall of China across the once beautiful valley where John Eliot's Praying Indians established the village of Nonantum in 1647. It was in this period that Boston College began filling in the smaller of the Chestnut Hill Reservoir's two basins.[21] Today, student housing and an assortment of college athletic and recreational facilities occupy a site whose "glimpses of deep blue water, and groves of trees and plots of green grass," historian S. F. Smith once described as a "perpetual benediction" to the area.[22] In the 1971 to 1977 period, Jewish Community Housing absorbed the 9-acre city yards between Chestnut Hill Avenue and Wallingford Road.[23] In the late seventies, Reservoir Towers, a 14-story structure, arose on a conspicuous V-shaped parcel of city parkland at the corner of Chestnut Hill Avenue and Commonwealth Avenue.[24]

Development also took its toll of historic landmarks. In the late fifties and early sixties—with the decline of movie-going due to the introduction of television—three theaters (The Allston (1955), Egyptian (1959) and Capitol (1962)) fell to wrecking crews. TV influenced Allston-Brighton positively as well. Since 1950 the North Brighton/North Allston area has become a major communications center, the home of WBZ-TV (Channel 4), WGBH-TV (Channel 2), and WSBK-TV (Channel 38).

The destruction of landmarks was not limited to out-moded movie palaces. A partial list of key buildings lost since 1963 includes the Warren School (1963), Brighton Stockyards (1967), Holton Library (1968), Union Hall (1969), Jackson School (1974), Brighton Town Hall (1976), Washington Allston School (1977), St. Margaret's Episcopal Church (1977), and the original St. Elizabeth's Hospital (1984).

In April 1965, *Citizen-Item* Editor Owen McNamara wrote bitterly of the lack of organized resistance to the forces generating physical blight, damaging development, and destruction of landmarks in Allston-Brighton. After listing some of Allston-Brighton contributions to history, McNamara concluded with the following powerful indictment of the prevailing attitude:

> We've lost it now. We trample on our past.
>
> We live in a certain house. On a certain street. In a certain section of the community. We are our certain selves, because that is all we can be sure of.
>
> Neighbors mean nothing—community means nothing. Past means nothing.
>
> Now to many people, Brighton's greatest virtue is that it is "handy." Handy to the stores. Handy to the shop or the office. The backbone of pride in community has been broken into thousands of bits and pieces: me, my car, my front yard, my house.
>
> This has to change if Allston-Brighton is to improve. A new sense of community will grow if a man's pride extends from his yard to his street, from his neighborhood to his city.
>
> Brighton's prideful past can provide the strong spine for the future.[25]

As the community's problems worsened from the mid-sixties onward, the more spirited residents began organizing. By the mid-seventies, Allston-Brighton had the city's largest population of civic groups.

The state of the public schools was a major issue in the sixties. Parents were concerned about the extremely poor physical condition of school buildings as well as the quality of the education their children were receiving in those buildings from the personnel of the conservative, patronage-ridden Boston Public Schools. When they tried

134

to secure improvements through the traditional medium of the Boston Home and School Association, they found it to be dominated by the school administration. As educational historian Peter Schrag noted of the Boston Home and School Association of the sixties, the group was uninterested in change and "wedded to the rest of the system."[26] Edythe York, a local leader characterized the organization as "political." It "never discussed educational or school problems," she asserted. "If an executive board began to discuss school problems or educational goals or grievances, the principal would get a new executive board."[27] Allston-Brighton's parents fought a vigorous, but ultimately unsuccessful battle to win control of the local chapters of the association. Failing in that goal, they resorted to organizing *ad hoc* committees.

The most significant of these groups was the Committee for a New Washington Allston which was founded in April 1966.[28] Its primary goal was the replacement of an 87-year-old structure, the oldest functioning school building in the city, with a modern facility. In time, however, the group embraced two additional concepts: the open classroom and the community school. Nine long years ensued before these aspirations were realized with the 1975 opening of the Jackson/Mann Community School in Union Square, Allston, a complex that combines a large, modern open classroom elementary school, a comprehensive facility for the deaf, and a community school offering a full range or programs to the general public.[29]

Owen McNamara concluded his 1965 editorial on the need for a stronger sense of community with the observation, "Brighton's prideful past can provide the strong spine for the future." Three years later, on April 1, 1968, the Brighton Historical Society held its first general meeting at the Faneuil Library in Oak Square. Appropriately, McNamara was the principal speaker of the occasion.[30] A key objective of the Brighton Historical Society has been the preservation and protection of the "physical and architectural resources of the community as embodied in its historical buildings, neighborhoods, monuments and landscapes."[31] In 1978 the society launched a major educational program—the Architectural Inventory Project—with the goal of raising public awareness of the community's rich architectural legacy.

An Architectural Inventory Team, consisting of neighborhood volunteers, compiled data on about 3,000 structures, developed slide presentations on the history of Allston-Brighton neighborhoods, and wrote a series of articles on the architectural history of the community. The 1979 designation of the Oak Square School as a City of Boston historic landmark stemmed from that effort.[32]

New civic and neighborhood organizations emerged in the post-1970 period: the Brighton/Allston Improvement Association, the Allston-Brighton Community Beautification Council, the Brighton/Washington Heights Citizens Association, the Washington Hill Civic Association; the Corey Hill Neighborhood Association, the South Allston Neighborhood Association, the Cleveland Circle Neighborhood Association, and the Allston-Brighton Community Development Corporation. Each group has made important contributions to the struggle against damaging zoning variances, increased liquor licenses, the loss of open space, institutional expansion, and myriad other threats to the quality of life in Allston-Brighton.

Greater ethnic diversity is another facet of contemporary Allston-Brighton. While the older ethnic groups—primarily Irish, Jews and Italians—continue to be represented in significant numbers, recent years have seen large numbers of Asians, Hispanics, and Blacks move into the community. As early as 1970 the local Spanish-speaking population stood at 300 families. Today Allston-

136

Children in front of Community Methodist Church, Washington Street, Brighton. On left Rev. Steven Griffith; on right Soeun Sorth (Cambodian minister).

Brighton has the highest concentration of Asians in Boston, a larger number than Chinatown. In 1980 the community contained 3,800 Asians, 2,900 Hispanics, and 2,700 Blacks.[33] To a greater extent, perhaps, than any other section of Boston, it has become a crossroads for people of diverse heritages. In sharp contrast to some parts of the city, moreover, it has established an admirable record for racial and ethnic harmony that is a source of genuine satisfaction to the community. An annual Allston-Brighton Parade and Ethnic Festival celebrates the ethnic and racial diversity of the neighborhood.

Since political powerlessness has been a major problem for decades, 1983 municipal charter reform guaranteeing Allston-Brighton representation on the Boston City Council and School Committee for the first time in thirty-two years must be regarded as a very hopeful sign. More importantly, Allston-Brighton has turned a corner—it has matured markedly as a community. New leadership has emerged. Activism has replaced indifference. A disposition to retreat before problems has given way to a spirit of determined resistance. In this writer's view, its prospects are today more hopeful than they have been for many years.

Notes

I. Establishing Little Cambridge (1630–1690)

    1. Francis Higginson, "New England Plantation," Perry Miller and Thomas H. Johnson (eds), *The Puritans: A Sourcebook of Their Writings*, I (New York: American Book Company, 1938), p. 123.

    2. Catherine Marten, *The Wampanoags in the Seventeenth Century: An Ethno-Historical Study* (Plimoth Plantation, 1970), *passim*; Alden T. Vaughan, *New England Frontier: Puritans and Indians, 1620–1672* (Boston: Little, Brown & Company), 1965, p. 54.

    3. Maud de Leigh Hodges, *Crossroads on the Charles: A History of Watertown, Massachusetts* (Watertown Free Public Library, 1980), p. 31.

    4. Lucius R. Paige, *History of Cambridge, Massachusetts, 1630–1877* (Boston: H. O. Houghton and Company, 1877), pp. 38–39; 624.

    5. Francis Jackson, *History of the Early Settlement of Newton, Massachusetts 1639–1800* (Boston: Stacy & Richards, 1854), p. 309; Paige, *History of Cambridge*, p. 587.

    6. John Eliot, "A True Revelation of our Beginnings with the Indians," *Collections of the Massachusetts Historical Society*, Third Series (1834), IV, p. 3.

    7. Ola E. Winslow, *John Eliot: "Apostle to the Indians"* (Boston: Houghton Mifflin Company, 1968), p. 101; Sarah S. Jacobs, *Nonantum and Natick* (Boston: Massachusetts Sunday School Society, 1853), *passim*.

    8. Jacobs, *Nonantum and Natick*, p. 53.

9. Jonathan Homer, "Description and History of Newton in the County of Middlesex," *Collections of the Massachusetts Historical Society for the Year 1798*, V, pp. 259–260.

10. Vaughan, *New England Frontier: Puritans and Indians, 1620–1675*, p. 318.

11. J.P.C. Winship, *Historical Brighton*, II (Boston, 1902), pp. 119–120.

12. Paige, *History of Cambridge*, pp. 399–400.

13. Michael McGiffer (ed.) *God's Plot: The Paradoxes of Puritan Piety: Being the Autobiography and Journal of Thomas Shepard* (University of Massachusetts Press, 1972) p. 60.

14. Frederick A. Whitney, *The Christian Mother: An Address Delivered at the Funeral of Mrs. Susanna (Park) Champney . . . Containing a Genealogical Notice of the Champney and Park Families* (Boston, 1855), pp. 16–18.

15. Elizabeth Ellery Dana, *The Dana Family in America* (Cambridge, 1956), pp. 35–48.

16. J.P.C. Winship, *Historical Brighton*, I (Boston, 1899), pp. 157–159.

17. Paige, *History of Cambridge*, pp. 502; 509; 618–19; 642; 655–56.

18. Dana, *The Dana Family in America*, pp. 38–39.

19. Lewis M. Hastings, "An Historical Account of Some Bridges Over Charles River," *Cambridge Historical Society Proceedings*, VII (April 1912), p. 53.

20. William P. Marchione, "Our Lost Waterways," *Historical Brighton* III (January 1979), pp. 6–8.

21. Frederick A. Whitney, "Brighton" Samuel Drake (ed.), *History of Middlesex County*, III, (Boston: Estes & Lauriat, 1889), pp. 290, 294; City of Boston, *A Record of the Streets, Alleys, Places, etc., in the City of Boston* (Boston, 1910), p. 486.

22. Paige, *History of Cambridge*, p. 37.

23. Lewis M. Hastings, "The Streets of Cambridge, Their Origin and History," *Cambridge Historical Society Proceedings* XIV (April, 1919), pp. 37–39.

24. Hastings, "Some Bridges Over the Charles River," pp. 54–56.

25. Paige, *History of Cambridge*, p. 442.

II.   Steps Toward Independence (1690–1790)

1. Paige, *History of Cambridge*, pp. 460–466.
2. S. B. Sutton, *Cambridge Reconsidered: 3½ Centuries on the Charles* (Cambridge 1976), pp. 1–2.
3. Paige, *History of Cambridge*, pp. 446–447.
4. Sutton, *Cambridge Reconsidered*, p. 23; Paige, *History of Cambridge*, pp. 132–133.
5. *Item*, July 20, 1889.
6. *Item*, August 3, 1889.
7. Frederick A. Whitney, "Brighton," Samuel A. Drake (ed), *History of Middlesex County, Massachusetts* I, pp. 290–296.
8. *Item*, March 6, 1886.
9. George B. Livermore, "Historical Paper," *The First Parish in Brighton: Historical Addresses* (Boston 1894), p. 34.
10. J.P.C. Winship, "Historical Address," *Brighton Day: Celebration of the One Hundredth Anniversary of the Incorporation of the Town of Brighton Held on August 3, 1907* (Boston, 1908), p. 44.
11. *Item*, July 20, 1889.
12. Francis S. Drake, "Brighton in the Provincial Period," Justin Winsor (ed.), *The Memorial History of Boston, 1630–1880* II (Boston: J.R. Osgood & Co., 1881), p. 372.
13. *Winning the Independence of Our Parish*, unsigned manuscript, May 12, 1929, Brighton Historical Society Archives, pp. 3–4; *Item*, August 10, 1889.
14. Livermore, "Historical Paper," pp. 32–42; Paige, *History of Cambridge*, pp. 294–296; for a list of the clergymen who preached in the Little Cambridge meeting-house prior to 1784 see *Item*, August 10, 1889.
15. Frederick A. Whitney, *An Address Delivered at the Consecration of Evergreen Cemetery, Brighton* (Boston, 1850), pp. 18–19.
16. John G. Curtis, *History of Brookline, Massachusetts* (Boston, 1933), p. 95.
17. Winship, *Historical Brighton* I, pp. 85–90.
18. "Thomas Gardner," *Appleton's Cyclopedia of American Biography* II, p. 598.
19. *Ibid.*

141

20. Richard Frothingham, *History of the Siege of Boston* (Boston: Little, Brown & Co., 1872), pp. 179–180.

21. Winship, *Historical Brighton* I, pp. 88–89.

22. William P. Cumming and Elizabeth C. Cumming, "The Treasure of Alnwick Castle," *American Heritage* XX (August 1969), p. 99; Drake, "Brighton in the Provincial Period," in Winsor (ed.), *The Memorial History of Boston, 1630–1880* IV, p. 371.

23. Curtis, *History of Brookline, Massachusetts*, p. 155.

24. "Winning the Independence of Our Parish," Unsigned manuscript, Brighton Historical Society Collection.

25. Mrs. John A. Weisse, *A History of the Bethune Family Together with a Sketch of the Faneuil Family* (1884), pp. 52–53.

26. Winship, *Historical Brighton* I, pp. 48–51.

27. Charles Hudson, *History of the Town of Lexington* II (Boston, 1913), pp. 762–775.

28. William Marchione, "The Smith-Winship House," *Historical Brighton* II (Summer, 1978), pp. 10–11.

29. Winship, *Historical Brighton* I, p. 124.

30. "Reminiscences," *Item*, August 31, 1886; William P. Marchione (ed.) "Brighton Center: 1820" (Merwin Reminiscences, Part II), *Historical Brighton* IV (Winter, 1981), pp. 10–11.

31. W. M. Cotton, "Brighton Fifty Years Ago: An Address Before the Faneuil Improvement Association," April 13, 1912, *Item*, April 20, 1912.

32. Williard M. Wallace, *Appeal to Arms: A Military History of the American Revolution* (Chicago: Quadrangle Books, 1964), p. 56.

33. Letter of Charles Miller to Major General Heath, June 22, 1777, Heath Collection, Massachusetts Historical Society.

34. Annie M. Judson, "The Captain Jonathan Winship Mansion," undated newspaper clippings in the Brighton Historical Society collection.

35. Victor S. Clark, *History of Manufactures in the United States*, I (New York, 1949), p. 482.

142

III. The Birth of Brighton (1790–1820)

1. Winship, *Historical Brighton* I, pp. 216–216.
2. Livermore, "Historical Paper," pp. 41–47.
3. Winship, *Historical Brighton* I, p. 216.
4. William S. Osborne (ed.), *The Power of Sympathy and the Coquette* (New Haven: College and University Press Services, Inc., 1970), p. 22.
5. Winship, *Historical Brighton* I, p. 217.
6. *Item*, September 4, 1886; William P. Marchione (ed.) "The Merwin Reminiscences, Part I, " *Historical Brighton: A Quarterly Publication of the Brighton Historical Society* III (April, 1980), pp. 8–9.
7. Paige, *History of Cambridge*, pp. 460–466.
8. Winship, *Historical Brighton* I, p. 200; Last Will and Testament of Stephen Dana, Docket 5862, Registry of Probate, Middlesex County, Massachusetts.
9. Paige, *History of Cambridge*, pp. 460–466.
10. Paige, *History of Cambridge*, p. 197.
11. Sutton, *Cambridge Reconsidered*, pp. 49–51.
12. "Remonstrance of the inhabitants of the towns of Newton and Cambridge to the Senate and House of Representatives of Massachusetts," January 28, 1792, Massachusetts State Archives.
13. Commonwealth of Massachusetts, *Acts of 1793*, Chapter 62, Massachusetts State Archives.
14. Paige, *History of Cambridge*, p. 203.
15. Cambridge Town Meeting Records, February 2, 1806.
16. Commonwealth of Massachusetts, *Acts of 1807*, Chapter 88, Massachusetts State Archives.
17. Cambridge town meeting records, April 6, 1806.
18. Cambridge town meeting records, June 6, 1806.
19. Commonwealth of Massachusetts, *Acts of 1807*.
20. J.P.C. Winship, "Historical Address," in *Brighton Day: Celebration of the One Hundreth Anniversary of the Incorporation of the Town of Brighton Held on August 3, 1907* (Boston: Municipal Printing Office, 1908), p. 53.

21. William P. Marchione, "The Parting of the Ways: Brighton's Separation from Cambridge in 1807," *Historical Brighton* IV (September, 1981), pp. 1–9.

22. Winship, *Historical Brighton* I, p. 126; Work Progress Administration, *Ships Registers and Enrollments of Boston and Charlestown* I, 1789–1795.

23. Rev. John Foster, *A Sermon Delivered May 16, 1803, the Sabbath After the Death of Captain Charles Winship who Died at St. Blas, December 4, 1800* (Boston, 1802), p. 10.

24. Hubert H. Bancroft, *History of Alaska, 1730–1885* (New York: Antiquarian Press Ltd., 1960), pp. 477–481; James Kirker, *Adventures to China: Americans in the Southern Oceans, 1792–1812* (New York: Oxford University Press, 1970), p. 153.

25. Hector Chevigny, *Lord of Alaska: The Story of Baranov and the Russian Adventure* (Portland, Oregon: Binfords & Mort, 1965), pp. 70–73; 184–185; 210–212; 223; 226; 238–244.

26. Winship, *Historical Brighton* I, pp. 127–128; *Solid Men of Boston in the North West* (unpublished manuscript in the Bancroft Library, University of California, n.d.) pp. 41–49. William Dana Phelps is believed to be the author of this highly detailed account of the Winship Family's activities in the Pacific. The Brighton Historical Society Collection contains a photocopy of the manuscript.

27. Dorothy Johansen and Charles Gates, *Empire of the Columbia: A History of the Pacific Northwest* (New York: Harper & Row, 1957), pp. 77–78; William P. Marchione, "The Remarkable Winships," *Historical Brighton* III (September, 1979), pp. 1–5.

28. Ralph S. Kuykendall, "Early Hawaiian Commercial Development," *Pacific Historical Review* III (1934), p. 370; Samuel Eliot Morison, "Boston Traders in the Hawaiian Islands, 1789–1828," *Washington Historical Quarterly* XII (July, 1921), p. 173.

29. Richard Tregaskis, *The Warrior King, Hawaii's Kamehameha the Great* (New York: Macmillan Publishing Co., Inc., 1973), p. 283.

30. Rev. and Mrs. Orramel Hincley Gulick, *The Pilgrims*

of Hawaii: *Their Own Story of Their Pilgrimage from New England and Life Work in the Sandwich Islands, Now Known as Hawaii* (New York: Fleming H. Revel Co., 1918), p. 81.

31. Winship, *Historical Brighton* I, pp. 128–130.

32. *Ibid*, p. 131.

33. *Ibid*, p. 130.

IV. The Flowering of Brighton (1820–1850)

1. Brighton Town Records, I, March 9, 1807.

2. Brighton Town Records, I, May 2, 1808; Winship "Historical Address," p. 45.

3. Livermore, "Historical Paper," p. 43.

4. *Ibid*, p. 46.

5. *Prospectus: Plans and Perspectives* (Brighton Evangelical Congregational Church, 1921), p. 5.

6. Livermore, "Historical Paper," p. 47.

7. Brighton Town Records, March 1, 1808.

8. Commonwealth of Massachusetts, Acts of 1808, Chapter 73.

9. Samuel A. Eliot (ed.), *Heralds of Liberal Faith, II: The Pioneers* (Boston: American Unitarian Association, 1910), pp. 36–37; William Marchione, "Noah Worcester: Brighton's Apostle of Peace," *Historical Brighton*, II (Fall, 1977), pp. 1–3.

10. Winship, *Historical Brighton*, I, pp. 37–41; "The First Mail," *Brighton Item*, April 2, 1887.

11. Winship, *Historical Brighton*, I, pp. 131–133.

12. Albert E. Benson, *History of the Massachusetts Horticultural Society* (Norwood, MA.: Plimpton Press, 1919), p. 522.

13. "Plan of the Winship Estate, Formerly Winship's Nurseries, Brighton, Mass." (May, 1856), Brighton Historical Society Collection.

14. Winship, *Historical Brighton*, I, pp. 193–195; Marshall P. Wilder, *The Horticulture of Boston and Vicinity* (Boston, 1881), pp. 58–59.

15. Winship, *Historical Brighton*, I, pp. 177–180; Benson, *History of the Massachusetts Horticultural Society*, pp. 122–136.

16. Wilder, *The Horticulture of Boston and Vicinity*, pp. 50–51.

17. Winship, *Historical Brighton*, I, p. 181.

18. Wilder, *The Horticulture of Boston and Vicinity*, pp. 50–51.

19. Winship, *Historical Brighton*, I, p. 181.

20. Wilder, *The Horticulture of Boston and Vicinity*, p. 50.

21. Winship, *Historical Brighton*, II, p. 209.

22. *An Outline of the History of the Massachusetts Society for Promoting Agriculture* (Boston: Meador Publishing Company, 1942), p. 17; *Massachusetts Agricultural Journal*, V (July, 1818), pp. 199–200; Harold U. Faulkner, *American Economic History* (New York: Harper & Brothers, 1960), p. 215.

23. *Brighton Town Records*, June 15, 1818.

24. *Brighton Town Records*, June, 1818; Winship, *Historical Brighton* I, p. 126.

25. *An Outline of the History of the Massachusetts Society for Promoting Agriculture*, p. 15.

26. *Ibid*, p. 17.

27. "Notices of the Brighton Cattle Show," *New England Farmer*, October 16, 1829 and October 23, 1829.

28. *An Outline of the History of the Massachusetts Society for Promoting Agriculture*, pp. 19–20.

29. "Plan of Land Appurtenant to the Agricultural Hall, Brighton to be Sold at Public Auction on the 23rd Day of October, 1844," Brighton Historical Society Collection.

30. "An Act to Unite the Watertown and Brighton Fisheries in Charles River, and for the Regulation and Management thereof," Chapter 76, *Acts and Resolves of the Commonwealth of Massachusetts*, February 21, 1827.

31. "Remonstrance Against Turnpike Prayed for by Gardner Green and others, Passing Through the Outskirts of the Town," *Brighton Town Records*, January 26, 1824.

32. "Report of the Directors of the Boston and Worcester Railroad Presented at a Special Meeting to the

Stockholders on January 18, 1833," *Boston Daily Advertiser and Patriot*, January 21, 1833.

33. Winship, *Historical Brighton*, I, p. 60.

34. "Reminiscences," *Brighton Item*, September 25, 1886.

35. Stephen Salisbury, *The State, the Investor, and the Railroad* (Cambridge: Harvard University Press, 1967), p. 99.

36. "The Cattle Fair Hotel and Cattle Trade," *Brighton Item*, July 27, 1889; Alvin F. Harlow, *Steelways of New England* (New York: Creative Age Press, Inc., 1946), pp. 96–98.

37. William Guild, *A Chart and Description of the Boston & Worcester and Western Railroads* (Boston: Bradbury and Guild, 1847), p. 15.

V. Brighton in the 1850s

1. George Adams, *A Business Directory of the Cities of Charlestown, Cambridge and Roxbury, and of the Towns of Chelsea, Somerville, Brighton, Brookline, Dorchester and Milton . . . with an Almanac for 1850* (Boston: Damrell & Moore, 1850), pp. 97–99.

2. John Hayward, *A Gazatteer of Massachusetts* (Boston: John Hayward, 1847), p. 114; Adams, *Almanac for 1850*, p. 101.

3. Nathaniel Hawthorne, *American Note Books*, in *Collected Works* (11th ed., 1887), IX, p. 248.

4. Broadside, "Cattle Fair Hotel," February 1834, Brighton Historical Society Collection.

5. Rochelle S. Elstein, "William Washburn and the Egyptian Revival in Boston," *Old Time New England: The Bulletin of the Society for the Preservation of New England Antiquities* LXX (1980), pp. 74–75; *Gleason's Pictorial Drawing Room Companion*, June 26, 1852, p. 409; "The Cattle Fair Hotel and Cattle Trade," *Item*, July 27, 1889.

6. Winship, *Historical Brighton*, I, p.. 111 and 114; Annie J. Judson, "The Captain Jonathan Winship Mansion: A Thing of the Past," Part III, *Item*, February 22, 1890.

7. Adams, *Almanac for 1850*, p. 93.

8. Bradley H. Clarke, "When the Trolleys Came to Brighton: a Lecture on the Historic Development of Public Transportation in Allston-Brighton," Brighton Historical Society, May 30, 1985.

9. Commonwealth of Massachusetts *Report of the Committee on Banks and Banking*, House 218, March 15, 1859.

10. Winship, *Historical Brighton*, I, p. 111; "The Brighton Market Bank," *Business History Society Bulletin* XII (April 1930), pp. 4–14.

11. Brighton Cooperative Bank, *Sixty-Five Years of Service*, 1911–1976 (1976).

12. Adams, *Almanac for 1850*, pp. 92–94; Jeremiah Spofford, *A Historical and Statistical Gazateer of Massachusetts* (Haverhill: E.G. Frothingham, 1860), p. 84.

13. *Ibid*, p. 101.

14. Frederick A. Whitney, *An Address Delivered at the Consecration of Evergreen Cemetery, Brighton, Wednesday, August 7, 1850, with an Appendix* (Boston).

15. *Annual Report of the School Committee of the Town of Brighton for 1847-48*, pp. 25–27.

16. *Annual Report of the School Committee of the City of Boston for 1902*, pp. 78–86.

17. Arthur Wellington Braley, *Schools and Schoolboys of Old Boston* (Boston: Louis P. Hager, 1944), pp. 22–23.

18. *Annual Report of the School Committee of the Town of Brighton for 1852-53*, p. 17.

19. *Brighton Town Records*, June 11, 1855.

20. J.P.C. Winship, "Brighton High School-House Dedication;" *Annual Report of the School Committee of the City of Boston for 1897*, p. 342.

21. J.P.C. Winship, "Brighton High School-House Dedication," pp. 338–341.

22. *Annual Report of the School Committee of the City of Boston for 1902*, pp. 78 and 86.

23. *Annual Report of the School Committee of the Town of Brighton for 1853-54*, p. 6.

24. *Annual Report of the School Committee of the Town of Brighton for 1851-52*, pp. 4–17.

25. *Annual Report of the School Committee of the Town of Brighton for 1848-49*, p. 23.

26. Francis S. Drake, "Brighton in the Last Hundred Years," *The Memorial History of Boston, 1630-1880*, III (Boston: James R. Osgood and Company, 1882), p. 606.

27. Adams, *Almanac for 1850*, p. 97.

28. *Prospectus: Plans and Perspectives* (Brighton Evangelical Congregationalist Church, 1921), p. 5.

29. *Item, December 11, 1943.*

30. Oscar Handlin, *Boston's Immigrants, 1790-1880* (New York: Atheneum, 1969) pp. 44-53.

31. "Census of the Inhabitants of the Town of Brighton," *Brighton Town Records*, July 12, 1855.

32. *Ibid.*

33. 1855 Census; also, *Item*, August 25, 1888. According to this article Thomas Brennan, Michael Coyle and Thomas Cochran had once been the only "Irishmen within (Brighton's) limits."

34. "List of the Taxpayers in Brighton for 1854," *Annual Report of the Receipts and Expenditures of the Town of Brighton for the Year Ending March 1, 1855*, pp. 17-35.

35. 1855 Census.

36. Handlin, *Boston's Immigrants*, pp. 199-201.

37. *Brighton Town Records*, November 13, 1854.

38. Sr. Marion Montague, *The History of St. Columbkille's Parish, 1850-1875*, unpublished manuscript, Brighton Historical Society Archives, p. 20.

39. St. Columbkille's Church Centennial Commission, *100th Anniversary, 1871-1971*; Montague, *The History of St. Columbkille's Parish, passim.*

40. *Ibid.*

41. *Brighton Town Records.*

VI.   The Critical Years (1860-1880)

1. Brighton Town Records, February 24, 1857.

2. Frederick A. Whitney, "Oration Delivered at the Dedication of the Soldiers' Monument in Evergreen

Cemetery, Brighton, Mass.," July 26, 1866, p. 47; *Item*, August 4, 1888.

3. Frederick A. Whitney, "Brighton," *History of Middlesex County*, p. 292.

4. Whitney, "Oration Delivered at the Dedication of the Soldier's Monument in Evergreen Cemetery, Brighton, Mass., " p. 40.

5. U.S. Bureau of the Census, *Eight and Ninth Censuses of the United States*, 1860 and 1870, Agricultural Schedules, Brighton, Massachusetts.

6. City of Boston, *Commissioner's Report on Annexation* (1873), Document 105, p. 5.

7. "Inauguration of the Bradlee Reservoir at Chestnut Hill," *Boston Daily Evening Traveller*, October 25, 1870, 4; Desmond Fitzgerald, *History of the Boston Water Works, 1868-1876* (Boston, 1876), p. 166.

8. Winship, *Historical Brighton*, II, p. 22.

9. City of Boston, *Annual Report of the Cochituate Water Works Board of the City of Boston for the Year Ending April 30, 1869*, Document 55, p. 41.

10. Winship, *Historical Brighton*, II, pp. 8-10.

11. S.F. Smith, *History of Newton, Massachusetts* (Boston, 1880), p. 38; William P. Marchione, "Building the Reservoir, 1866-1870," *Historical Brighton*, II (Winter 1978), pp. 1-3.

12. "Letter from Uriel H. Crocker to the Committee of the City Government on the Subject of a Public Park," City Document 123, pp. 87-95; Cynthia Zaitzevsky, *Frederick Law Olmsted and the Boston Park System* (Cambridge: Harvard University Press, 1982), p. 36.

13. *Boston Transcript*, May 17, 1910; Robert F. Needham, "Vermont Susquicentennial Recalls Universalist Minister," clipping in the Brighton Historical Society Archives, March 22, 1941.

14. Winship, *Historical Brighton* II, pp. 81-82.

15. Frederic A. Whitney, "Brighton," *History of Middlesex County* I, p. 290.

16. Winship, *Historical Brighton* I, p. 226.

17. Whitney, "Brighton," *History of Middlesex County* I, p. 290.

18. St. Columbkille's Church Centennial Commission, *100th Anniversary, 1871-1971*, pp. 8-9.

19. W.M. Cotton, "Brighton Fifty Years Ago: An Address Before the Faneuil Improvement Association April 13, 1862"; *Item*, April 20, 1912, 1.

20. Adams, *Almanac for 1850*, pp. 98-99.

21. *Item*, April 24, 1886.

22. U.S. Bureau of the Census, *Eighth Census of the United States*, 1860, Manufacturing Schedule, Brighton, Massachusetts.

23. Town of Brighton, *Inspection of the Slaughterhouses of Brighton on April 30, 1866 by Henry G. Clark, M. D. of Boston* (1866), pp. 6-12.

24. Town of Brighton, *Inspection of the Slaughterhouses of Brighton* (1866), pp. 6-12; Henry M. Wightman, *Plan of the Town of Brighton* (1866), Massachusetts State Archives.

25. Town of Brighton, *Report of the Board of Health for the Year Ending January 31, 1867* (1867), pp. 52-53.

26. Town of Brighton, "Extract from Report of State Board of Health on Slaughtering for the Boston Market," *Report of the Board of Health for the Year Ending January 31, 1870* (1870), p. 61.

27. *Ibid*, pp. 64-65.

28. Town of Brighton, "Registry of Deaths," *Official Reports of the Town of Brighton for the Year Ending January 31, 1870* (1870), pp. 91-97.

29. Town of Brighton, *Report of the Board of Health* (1870), p. 65.

30. Commonwealth of Massachusetts, "Laws Regarding the Abattoir," *Report of the State Board of Health* (January 1878), p. 13.

31. *Arguments Before the Joint Committee on Mercantile Affairs . . . for an Act to Incorporate the Massachusetts Abattoir Company, April 25, 1872* (1872), p. 11.

32. Winship, *Historical Brighton II*, pp. 187-188.

33. *Brighton Town Records*, March 14, 1870.

34. *Brighton Town Records*, March 11, 1872.

35. "A Specimen Reformer," *Boston Daily Advertiser*, October 31, 1876.

36. Town of Brighton, *Treasurer's Report of the Expenditures and Receipts of the Town of Brighton*, 1870–1873.

37. William P. Marchione, *Brighton's Annexation to Boston: A Talk Given Before the Brighton Historical Society, October 29, 1984*, Brighton Historical Society Archives.

38. Town of Brighton, *Proceedings of the Town Meetings*, June 14, 1873.

39. St. Columbkille's Church Centennial Commission, *100th Anniversary 1871–1971*, p. 3.

40. City of Boston, *Proceedings of the Common Council*, January 22, 1874.

41. *Brighton Messenger*, January 24, 1874, 2.

42. *Brighton Town Records*, January 10, 1872.

43. Petition of George A. Wilson and Others for the Annexation of the Town of Brighton to the City of Boston, January 25, 1872, Massachusetts State Archives.

44. Petition of Abiel Rice and Others Against the Annexation of the Town of Brighton to the City of Boston, February 26, 1872, Massachusetts State Archives.

45. *Brighton Town Records*, December 20, 1872.

46. *Brighton Town Records*, October 7, 1873.

47. William P. Marchione, "Annexation: A Closer Look," *Historical Brighton: A Quarterly Publication of the Brighton Historical Society* II (Spring 1978), pp. 1–5.

48. Roger Lane, *Policing the City: Boston, 1822–1885* (New York: Atheneum, 1971), pp. 177–178.

49. Winship, II, p. 102; City of Boston, *Annual Report of the School Committee of the City of Boston, 1902*, p. 78.

50. *Ibid*, p. 85.

51. Walter Muir Whitehill, *Boston Public Library: A Centennial History* (Cambridge: Harvard University Press, 1956), p. 87.

52. City of Boston, *Proceedings of the School Committee*, April 13, 1880, pp. 80–81, 96.

VII.   Streetcar Suburb (1880–1915)

1. Sam Bass Warner, Jr., *Streetcar Suburbs; The Process of Growth in Boston, 1870–1900* (New York: Atheneum, 1971), p. 22.

2. "Plan of Valuable House Lots for Sale on the Cattle Fair Hotel Grounds," (April, 1884), Brighton Historical Society Archives.

3. Kenneth Lewis, *Livestock Marketing and Meat Packing* (M.B.A. Thesis, Northeastern University, 1954), pp. 5–8.

4. George W. and Walter S. Bromley, *Atlas of the City of Boston: Brighton* (Philadelphia: G. W. Bromley & Co., 1916), Plate 15; *Boston City Directory for 1916* (Boston: Sampson & Murdock Co., 1916).

5. Philip Taylor, *The Distant Magnet: European Emigration to the U.S.A.* (New York: Harper & Row, 1971), p. 214.

6. Boston Landmarks Commission, *Allston-Brighton Preservation Survey* (1978), Survey Form AB9.

7. Helen Swift, *My Father and My Mother* (Chicago: n.d.), pp. 19–21; New York Times, March 30, 1903, 1 and April 9, 1903, 5.

8. Winship, *Historical Brighton* II, pp. 15–16.

9. Louis P. Hager, *History of the West End Street Railway* (Boston, 1891), p. 13; Boston Street Railway Association, *A Chronicle of the Boston Transit System* (1981).

10. *Atlas of Suffolk County*, VII: Brighton, Massachusetts (Philadelphia: G.M. Hopkins & Co., 1875), Plate M; *Atlas of the City of Boston*, VI: Charlestown and Brighton (Philadelphia: G.W. Bromley & Co. 1885), Plates I and H; *Atlas of the City of Boston*, VII: Brighton (Philadelphia: G. W. Bromley & Co., 1890), Plates 7 & 26.

11. Henry-Russell Hitchcock, *The Architecture of H. H. Richardson and His Times* (Hamden, Conn.: Archon Books, 1971), pp. 224–225.

12. *Item*, March 14, 1891 and August 8, 1891.

13. *Item*, May 2, 1891.

14. Boston Landmarks Commission, Allston-Brighton Preservation Survey (1978), Survey Form AB 406.

15. John W. Linnehan and Edward E. Cogswell, *The Driving Clubs of Greater Boston* (Boston, 1914), p. 133.

16. *Item*, November 16, 1903.

17. *Item*, June 24, 1944.

18. *Item*, August 7, 1886.

19. John Gould Curtis, History of the Town of Brookline, Massachusetts (New York: Houghton Mifflin Co., 1933), p. 300.

20. Item, September 3, 1887; City of Boston, Annual Report of the Street Department (1892–95).

21. Item, August 9, 1890.

22. Boston Landmarks Commission, Allston-Brighton Preservation Survey (1978), Survey Form AB 1022.

23. Cynthia Zaitzevsky, Frederick Law Olmsted and the Boston Park System (Cambridge: Harvard University Press, 1982), pp. 111.

24. Atlas of Dorchester, West Roxbury and Brighton, City of Boston (Boston: J. P. Brown & Co., 1899), Plates 34, 36, 38 and 40; George W. and Walter S. Bromley, Atlas of the City of Boston: Ward 25, Brighton (Philadelphia: G. W. Bromley & Co., 1905, 1916), Plates 7–11; 16–18 and 24.

25. Item, May 9, 1891.

26. Item, July 9, 1892.

27. Ibid.

28. Item, September 12, 1891 and June 16, 1892.

29. Item, May 19, 1888 and January 6, 1894.

30. City of Boston, Report of the City Architect for 1894, pp. 10–13.

31. Item, September 19, 1896.

32. Atlas of Dorchester, West Roxbury and Brighton (1899), Plate 37.

33. Winship, Historical Brighton, II, pp. 28–29.

34. Winship, Historical Brighton, I, p. 101.

35. Item, March 8, 1890.

36. Item, December 28, 1889.

37. Item, April 5, 1890.

38. Ibid.

39. Item, May 17, 1890.

40. Item, June 14, 1890.

41. Atlas of Dorchester, West Roxbury and Brighton (1899), Plate 33: Atlas of the City of Boston: Ward 25, Brighton (1909, 1916), Plate 16.

42. City of Boston, Annual Report of the Street Department for 1894 (1895), p. 94.

43. *Ibid.*, p. 96.

44. William P. Marchione, "Draining Brighton's Marshes," *Historical Brighton* II (Summer, 1978), pp. 5–9.

45. Commonwealth of Massachusetts, *Report of the Joint Board Consisting of the Metropolitan Park Commission and the State Board of Health upon the Improvement of Charles River* (April, 1894), pp. 6–7.

46. Charles W. Eliot, *Charles Eliot: Landscape Architect* (Boston, 1902), pp. 588–589; Robert E. Barrett, "A Resume of the Charles River Basin Project," *Harvard Engineering Journal* (January, 1907), pp. 145–156.

47. Commonwealth of Massachusetts, *Charles River Dam: Evidence and Arguments Before the Board of Harbor and Land Commissioners* (1903).

48. Linnehan, *The Driving Clubs of Greater Boston*, pp. 33–60.

49. Henry Lee Higginson, "The Soldier's Field," *Four Addresses* (Boston, 1892).

50. Boston Landmarks Commission, *Allston-Brighton Preservation Survey* (1978), Forms AB 525 and AB 526.

51. Melvin T. Copeland, *And Mark an Era: The Story of the Harvard Business School* (Boston: Little Brown & Co., 1958), pp. 71–74.

52. *Boston Traveller*, March 31, 1967, 3.

53. John E. Sexton and Arthur J. Riley, *History of St. John's Seminary, Brighton* (Boston; Roman Catholic Archbishop of Boston, 1945), pp. 53–55.

54. *Item* October 11, 1890 and June 13, 1891.

55. *Item*, February 15, 1908.

56. Dorothy G. Wayman, *Cardinal O'Connell of Boston* (New York: Farrar Straus & Young, 1955) p. 187; *Twenty-Five Years, 1911–1936: Silver Jubilee of St. Gabriel Laymen's Retreat League* (Brighton, 1963), pp. 14–19.

57. *Allston-Brighton Preservation Survey* (1978) Survey Form AB 515.

58. *Allston-Brighton Preservation Survey* (1978), Survey Form AB 510.

59. St. Elizabeth's Hospital, *One Hundred Years of Service 1869–1969.* ·

60. "St. Columbkilles is Mother of 4 Parishes," *Boston Traveler*, March 21, 1967.

61. *Item*, September 27, 1890.

62. *Dedication Program, First Parish Church in Brighton, March 31, 1895*, Brighton Historical Society Archives.

63. Grace Whiting Myers, *History of St. Luke's Church in Allston* (1934)

64. *Allston-Brighton Preservation Survey* (1978), *passim*.

VIII. The Yankee Exodus (1910–1930)

1. City of Boston, *Annual Reports of the Board of Election Commissioners* (1910, 1930).

2. City of Boston, *Annual Report of the Board of Election Commissioners for the Year 1909*.

3. William L. O'Connell, *Everyone Was Brave: A History of Feminism in America* (Chicago: Quadrangle Books, 1969), pp. 84–86.

4. Isabella H. Williams, *A History of the Brighthelmstone Club of Brighton and Allston* (Cambridge: The University Press, n.d.) pp. 3–7; 139.

5. John F. Stack, Jr., *International Conflict in an American City: Boston's Irish, Italians, and Jews, 1935–1944* (Westport, Cn.: Greenwood Press, 1979), p. 42.

6. *Item*, June 13, 1925.

7. "Constitution," Faneuil Improvement Association Collection, Brighton Historical Society Archives.

8. "Members, 1919," Faneuil Improvement Association Collection, Brighton Historical Society Archives.

9. *Boston City Directory* (1910).

10. "Constitution," Faneuil Improvement Association Collection, Brighton Historical Society Archives.

11. "Secretary's Annual Report," December 9, 1911, Faneuil Improvement Association, Brighton Historical Society Archives.

12. "Undated newspaper clipping" (1910), Faneuil Improvement Association Collection, Brighton Historical Society Archives.

13. *Boston Globe*, February 16, 1947, 1.

14. William P. Marchione, "The 1949 Boston Charter Reform," *New England Quarterly* 49 (September, 1976): 374.

15. City of Boston, *Annual Report of the Board of Election Commissioners for the Year 1909.*

16. Andrew Buni and Alan Rogers, *Boston: City on a Hill* (Woodland Hills, Cal.: Windsor Publications, 1984). pp. 110-111.

17. *Item,* January 8, 1910.

18. Stack, *International Conflict in an American City,* p. 83.

19. *Item,* April 17, 1909.

20. *Item,* December 18, 1909.

21. *Item,* December 25, 1909.

22. City of Boston, Annual Report of the Board of Election Commissioners for the Year 1910.

23. City of Boston, *List of Requests for Local Improvements* (Document 51, 1910), pp. 24-28.

24. City of Boston, *The Advance of Boston: A Pictorial Review of the Municipal Progress of this City During the Years 1910-1913* (1913), *passim.*

25. City of Boston, *Annual Report of the Board of Election Commissioners for the Year 1914.*

26. Thomas H. O'Connor, *Bibles, Brahmins and Bosses: A Short History of Boston* (Boston: Trustees of the Boston Public Library, 1976), p. 122.

27. *Item,* July 27, 1914.

28. City of Boston, *Proceedings of the City Council,* September 11, 1911; January 5, 1914; April 13, 1914; May 17, 1915; and February 5, 1917.

29. "Resolution of the Faneuil Men's Club . . . Toward the Improvement of Brooks Street" (May 19, 1919), Faneuil Improvement Association Collection, Brighton Historical Society Archives.

30. *Atlas of the City of Boston* (Philadelphia, G.W. Bromley & Co., 1925) Plates 1, 3 & 13.

31. Letter from the Faneuil Improvement Association to Mayor Andrew J. Peters, October 22, 1919, Faneuil Improvement Association Collection, Brighton Historical Society Archives.

32. "Volunteers for Patrol Service," Faneuil Improvement Association, Brighton Historical Society Archives.

33. *Atlas of the City of Boston* (Philadelphia: G. W. Bromley & Co., 1925), Plates 1, 2, 3, 4 and 6.

34. *Directory of the City of Boston* (1910, 1930).

35. *Item*, September 8, 1923.

36. City of Boston, *Annual Report of the Board of Election Commissioners* (1910, 1930).

37. *Directory of the City of Boston* (1910, 1930).

38. Ben Rosen, *The Trend of Jewish Population in Boston: A Study to Determine the Location of a Jewish Communal Building* (Boston: Federated Jewish Charities, 1921), p. 16.

39. City of Boston, *Officials and Employees of the City of Boston and the County of Suffolk with their Residences, Compensation, etc., 1919.*

40. *Atlas of the City of Boston* (Philadelphia: G. W. Bromley & Co., 1925) Plates 10, 11, 16, 17, 18 and 24.

41. *Item*, March 27, 1917.

42. *Directory of the City of Boston* (1920, 1930).

43. *Directory of the City of Boston* (1928-1940).

44. *Item*, February 10, 1983.

45. John Simons (ed.), *Who's Who in American Jewry: A Biographical Dictionary of Living Jews of the United States and Canada, 1938-1939* (New York: Nationalities Association, Inc., 1938), p. 388.

46. *Boston Evening Globe*, March 28, 1969, 35.

47. City of Boston, *Annual Reports of the Board of Election Commissioners* (1901-1909).

48. City of Boston, *Annual Report of the Board of Election Commissioners for the Year 1910.*

49. City of Boston, *Annual Report of the Board of Election Commissioners for the Year 1916.*

50. *Atlas of the City of Boston* (Philadelphia: G. W. Bromley & Co., 1925), Plates 12, 15 and 21.

51. *Item*, July 10, 1926.

52. *Item*, August 1, 1925.

53. Charles A. and Mary R. Beard, *The Rise of American Civilization* (New York: The Macmillan Company, 1927), p. 636.

54. *Item*, April 14, 1917.

55. *Item*, May 19, 1917 and June 30, 1917.

56. Williams, *A History of the Brighthelmstone Club*, pp. 107-115: *Item*, June 16, 1917.

57. *Item*, July 17, 1917.

58. *Item*, September 27, 1917.

59. *Item*, November 16, 1918.

60. *Item*, November 16, 1918.

61. Boston Landmarks Commission, *Allston-Brighton Neighborhood Survey* (1979).

62. Dorothy G. Wayman, *Cardinal O'Connell of Boston*, pp. 183-195.

63. *Item*, January 29, 1927.

IX. The Great Depression—World War II—
Post-War Development (1930-1960)

1. City of Boston, *Annual Report of the Board of Election Commissioners for the Year 1950*.

2. *Brighton Citizen*, April 2, 1959, 1.

3. *Brighton Citizen*, January 27, 1955, 1.

4. *Item*, November 27, 1937: Katie Kenneally, *Brighton* (Boston 200 Neighborhood Histories Series, 1975), pp. 18-19.

5. City of Boston, *Tercentenary of the Founding of Boston, 1630-1930* (1930), p. 275.

6. Boston Landmarks Commission, *Allston-Brighton Neighborhood Survey* (1979), AB 512.

7. *Directory of the City of Boston* (1929-1932).

8. *Item*, July 20, 1935.

9. *Item*, July 20, 1935.

10. Charles H. Trout, *Boston, The Great Depression and the New Deal* (New York: Oxford University Press, 1977), p. 85.

11. *Item*, July 20, 1935.

12. "One Hundreth Anniversary Supplement," *Item*, August 17, 1984, 2.

13. *Item*, January 18, 1935; October 25, 1941.

14. *Brighton Citizen*, June 7, 1956, 1.

15. *Item*, December 18, 1937; *Item*, December 7, 1940; *Citizen*, October 9, 1941.

16. *Item*, December 18, 1937; *Item*, December 7, 1940; *Citizen*, October 9, 1941.

17. City of Boston, *Lists of Requests for Public Improvements* (1910), p. 28: *Item*, March 5, 1921 and April 23, 1921; *Item*, March 22, 1941.

18. *Item*, December 13, 1941.

19. *Ibid.*

20. *Ibid.*

21. *Brighton Citizen*, May 11, 1950, 1.

22. *Item*, November 30, 1935.

23. *Brighton Citizen*, May 24, 1951, 1.

24. *Brighton Citizen*, March 9, 1950, 1 and June 29, 1950, 1.

25. *Brighton Citizen*, June 6, 1950, 1.

26. City of Boston, Annual Report of the City Planning Board for 1946 (1947), p. 9.

27. William P. Marchione, "The 1949 Boston Charter Reform," *New England Quarterly, passim.*

28. *Brighton Citizen*, July 28, 1955, 1.

29. *Item*, January 16, 1926.

30. *Brighton Citizen*, February 6, 1958, 5; May 29, 1958, 1.

31. *Brighton Citizen*, December 17, 1959, 1 and March 24, 1960, 1.

32. *Brighton Citizen*, December 17, 1959, 1 and March 24, 1960, 1.

33. *Brighton Citizen*, April 22, 1948, 1.

34. *Brighton Citizen*, April 22, 1948, 1; August 15, 1957, 7; March 17, 1949, 1; April 21, 1949, 1.

35. *Brighton Citizen*, January 15, 1959, 1.

36. *Brighton Citizen*, February 19, 1953, 1.

37. *Brighton Citizen*, July 24, 1952, 1; January 28, 1954, 1.

38. *Brighton Citizen*, February 28, 1957, 1.

39. *Brighton Citizen*, April 7, 1955, 1.

40. *Brighton Citizen*, October 31, 1957, 1.

41. *Brighton Citizen*, February 13, 1958, 1.

42. *Allston Citizen*, April 24, 1947, 1 and December 8, 1949, 1.

43. *Item*, June 10, 1944; City of Boston, *Annual Report of the Board of Election Commissioners* (1940–1948).
44. *Brighton Citizen*, December 20, 1951, 1.
45. Brigite S. Grossman, *Experiencing Jewish Boston: A Self-Guided Tour* (Boston: Jewish Community Center of Greater Boston, 1981), p. 31; *Brighton Citizen*, January 4, 1951, 1.
46. *Allston Citizen*, September 18, 1947, 1.
47. *Brighton Citizen*, September 8, 1949, 1.

X. The Years Since 1960

1. Boston Planning Board, *Annual Report for the Year Ending December 31, 1951* (1952), p. 24; Boston Redevelopment Authority, *Allston-Brighton District Profile and Proposed 1979–1981 Neighborhood Improvement Program* (1979), p. 3.
2. Boston Redevelopment Authority, *Boston Population and Housing by Neighborhood Areas, 1980: Demographic Information from the U.S. Bureau of the Census* (1983), Table P-1.
3. Whitehill, *Boston: A Topographical History*, pp. 213–232; *Brighton Citizen-Item*, February 16, 1961, 1.
4. *Item*, July 20, 1935; Boston Redevelopment Authority, *Boston Population and Housing by Neighborhood Areas, 1980*, Table P-1.
5. *Boston Globe, Boston: A Closeup of Its Neighborhoods, Its People and Its Problems* (1967), 5.
6. *Allston-Brighton Citizen-Item*, February 9, 1967, 1 and November 30, 1976, 1.
7. *Brighton Citizen-Item*, September 28, 1961, 1.
8. *Brighton Citizen-Item*, March 2, 1961, 1; July 12, 1962, 1; September 10, 196?.
9. Boston Redevelopment Authority, *Allston Brighton District Profile*, 1979–1981, p. 4; *Brighton Citizen-Item*, June 6, 1963, 4.
10. *Brighton Citizen-Item*, June 8, 1961, 1; October 4, 1962.

11. *Allston Citizen Item*, December 16, 1962, 1; *Brighton Citizen-Item*, January 3, 1963, 1 and January 17, 1963, 1; *Allston-Brighton Citizen Item*, July 22, 196?, 1; August 19, 1965, 1 and October 14, 1965, 1.

12. *Allston-Brighton Citizen Item*, June 27, 1968, 1.

13. *Allston-Brighton Citizen Item*, August 8, 1964, 1.

14. *Allston-Brighton Citizen Item*, September 3, 1964; August 12, 1965, 1.

15. *Allston-Brighton Citizen-Item*, October 14, 1965, 1.

16. *Allston-Brighton Citizen-Item*, September 1, 1966, 1.

17. *Allston-Brighton Citizen-Item*, October 23, 1969, 23.

18. *Brighton Citizen-Item*, February 19, 1953, 1; April 14, 1960, 1; April 3, 1958, 1.

19. Reed Ueda, *West End House* (Boston: West End House, 1981), pp. 149–150.

20. *Allston-Brighton Citizen-Item*, August 11, 1966, 1.

21. *Brighton Citizen-Item*, February 16, 1961, 1; *Allston-Brighton Citizen-Item*, August 27, 1970, 1.

22. S. F. Smith, *History of Newton, Massachusetts* (Boston, 1880), p. 735.

23. *Allston-Brighton Citizen-Item*, August 17, 1970, 1.

24. *Allston-Brighton Citizen-Item*, January 1, 1976, 1.

25. *Allston-Brighton Citizen-Item*, April 1, 1965, 8.

26. Peter Schrag, *Village School Downtown* (Boston: Beacon Press, 1967), p. 139.

27. Edythe B. York, *The Neighborhood School and Politics* (1975), unpublished manuscript, Brighton Historical Society Archives.

28. *Allston-Brighton Citizen-Item*, April 28, 1966, 8.

29. *Allston-Brighton Citizen-Item*, February 5, 1976, 1.

30. *Allston-Brighton Citizen-Item*, March 28, 1968.

31. Statement of Purpose, *Brighton Historical Society By-Laws*.

32. Brighton Historical Society, Architectural Inventory File.

33. Boston Redevelopment Authority, *Boston Population and Housing by Neighborhood Area*, 1980, Table P-1.

Index

A

Aberdeen Civic and Improvement
  Association, 120, 124
Aberdeen section of Brighton, 88–89
Academy Hill Road, 22, 26, 58, 60, 90
Adams, Charles Francis, 88
Agricultural Hill, 45
Agriculture, 12, 44–45, 69. See also
  Horticulture
Aharath Achim congregation, 108
Ahearn, Francis X., 121
Alaskan trade, 32–34
Alexander Hamilton School, 113
Algonquian language, 4
Alice Gallagher Park, 118
Allston-Brighton Community
  Beautification Council, 136
Allston-Brighton Community
  Development Corporation, 136
Allston Civic Association, 128–129
Allston Grammar School. See
  Washington Allston Grammar School
Allston Hall, 86
Allston, North. See *North Allston*
Allston post office, 73
Allston railroad depot, 72, 75, 86
Allston Square, 83
Allston Street, 41, 60, 94, 97
Allston Theater, 111, 114, 133
American Party. See *Know Nothing
  Party*
American Peace Movement, 39. See also
  Massachusetts Peace Society
American Revolution, 16–23
Andrew Jackson School, 113, 133
Annexation of Brighton to Boston,
  79–80, 82
Anti-Irish sentiment. See *Irish,
  prejudice against*

Appleton, Dr. Nathan, 15
Archbishop's residence, 113
Armenian population, 110
Asian population, 136–137
Aspinwall Woods, 57
Austen, Jonathan Loring, 38
Automobile industry, 116
Automobiles, effects on Brighton, 116,
  123, 127

B

Back Bay, 10, 46–47, 69, 72
Baker, Benjamin, 29, 70
Baker Library, 96
Baldwin, Henry, 58
Baldwin, Life, 56
Bank of Brighton, 56
Banks and banking, 56. See also
  individual banks
Baptist Society, 61
Baptists, 61, 98
Baranov, Alexander, 32–33
Barrett Elementary School, 116
Barron, Jennie Loitman, 109
Barry's Corner, 129–131
Baxter, Horace W., 76–77
Baxter's Place, 74
Beacon Hill, 69
Beacon Park Raceway, 87
Beacon Street, 70, 85, 88–89
Bears in Cambridge, 13
Beatty's Ledge, 90
Beef. See *Cattle industry*
Beire, Rev. P. O., 65
Bellvue, 64
Benedetto Viola Square, 110
Bennett Grammar School, 81–82
Bennett, Stephen Hastings, 81
Bennett (Stephen Hastings) House, 84

Fitzgerald, John "Honey Fitz," 103–104
Flood, Father, 64
Flynn, Patrick, 65
Fort Ticonderoga, 20
Foster, Hannah, 25–26
Foster, Rev. John, 16, 25–26, 36–38
Foster Street, 26, 39, 63, 74, 96
Francis, Ebenezer, 88
Franciscan Sisters of Africa
  Convent, 26
Franklin Street, 86, 110
The Friends of Peace, 39
Frothingham, Richard, 18
Fuller, George F., 72, 82
Fuller, Granville A., 50

G

Gannett, Caleb, 30
Gardner, Elizabeth, 17
Gardner family, 13, 15
Gardner, Henry J., 64
Gardner, John, 16
Gardner, Massachusetts, 19
Gardner, Richard, 17
Gardner Street, 86
Gardner, Thomas, 17–19, 26, 29
Gardner, Thomas, Jr., 36
Gem, 87
General Court, Massachusetts, 8–10,
  15–17, 25–27, 29–31, 36, 130
General Federation of Women's
  Clubs, 100
Glenville Avenue, 124
Goding's Hotel, 55
Good Government Association, 102
Goodenough, Henry, B., 94, 97
Gookin, Daniel, 3, 6
Gordon Street, 58
Graham, Edward F., 98
Grape culture, 43
Graves, Rev. Joseph M., 61
Gray, Horace, 41–44
Grazing, 2, 13, 22
The Great Bridge, 7, 11, 19, 27, 31
Greek population, 110
Griggs family, 15

Griggs, Moses, 16
Griggs, Nathaniel, 61

H

Hano, Samuel, 86
Hano Street, 86
Hanoville district, 128
Hardy, Dudley, 36
Harriet Baldwin School, 113
Harvard Avenue, 17, 72, 86, 88–89
  114, 124
Harvard Bridge, 70
Harvard Business School, 96
Harvard College, 12–13, 25, 30, 58, 77
Harvard Square, 9, 15–16, 19
Harvard Stadium, 96, 119
Harvard Street, 10, 85, 108
Harvard University, 96, 127
Hasiotis Funeral Home, 89
Hastings Tavern, 45
Hathaway, James A., 85
Hathaway (James A.) mansion, 84
Hawaiian Islands, trade with, 34–35
Hawthorne, Nathaniel, 50, 55
Heath, Elder, 3
Henshaw Street, 92
Higgins Street, 17
Higginson, Rev. Francis, 1
Hildreth, Hosea, 58
Hill, Aaron, 30
Hill, Benjamin, 36
Hill Memorial Baptist Church, 98
Hispanic population, 136–137
Holley, Elizabeth, 3
Holley family, 2
Holley, Samuel, 3
Holmes, Dr. Oliver Wendell, 25, 60
Holton, James, 82
Holton Library, 81 (illus.), 82, 133
Homer and Winship, firm of, 31
Homer, Benjamin, 31
Homer, Rev. Jonathan, 5
Horse market, 51
Horse racing, 87, 96
Horticulture, 35, 39, 41–43, 56
House of Representatives, 28

Howe, Albert, 65
Hunt, Thomas, 56
Husbandry, 44
Hyde Park, 120

I

Indians, 1-7, 33-34. See also
    "Praying Indians"
Inman family, 13
Ireland, 61-62
Irish population, 61-63, 65, 100-101,
    103-104, 107, 136
Irish, prejudice against, 63-64
Italian population, 100, 110, 136
Item, 72, 87-90, 92-94, 112, 115, 117

J

Jackson, Andrew, 65
Jackson, Edward, 3, 8-9
Jackson/Mann Community School, 135
Jackson, William Henry, 70
James A. Garfield School, 113
Jewish population, 84, 100, 108-110,
    124-125, 133, 136
Jordan, Horace W., 76-77, 80

K

Kadimah-Toras Moshe congregation,
    125
Kamehameha I, 34-35
Katkoff, Rabbi Moses, 84
Kauma-lii, 34
Kehillath Israel congregation, 108
Keith, Benjamin F., 113
Kendall, John, 3
Kenmore Square, 46
Kennedy Memorial Hospital, 90, 125
Kennedy, Rose Fitzgerald, 101
Kenny, Thomas, 104
Kenrick Street, 118, 121
King Philip's War, 6
Knapp, Jacob, 58
Knight, Rev. Cyrus F., 71
Know Nothing Party, 63-64

Knowles, John H., 104
Knox, Colonel Henry, 20

L

Lafayette, General, 55
Lake Shore Road, 118
Lake Street, 41, 96, 98, 132
Lanark Street, 89
Land use, 69, 83, 85-86, 88-89, 93-94
    120, 122
Lawrence, Abbott, 46
Lawrence, Amos, 70
Lawrence Basin, 70
Lawrence Place, 108
Lechmere family, 13
Lee, Alderman John, 92
Lee, General Arthur, 21
Leo Birmingham Parkway, 117, 119
Lexington, 19, 22
Lincoln Street, 84, 111, 129
Linden Street, 86
Little Cambridge, 6-17, 19-20, 22,
    24-31
Little Cambridge Cattle Market.
    See *Cattle Market*
Little Cambridge Meetinghouse, 15
Lithuanian population, 84, 110
Livermore, George B., 14
Livermore, Jonathan, 36
Lobel, Louis, 125
Longfellow Bridge, 70
Longfellow, Henry Wadsworth, 41
    95, 112
Lyceum Movement, 60

M

Maginnis and Walsh, 97-98
Malbert Road, 62, 84
Mann, Horace, 58
Manufacturing industries, 56
Mapleton Street, 92
Market Square, 55
Market Street, 8, 10, 13-14, 39-40, 55,
    62, 65, 84, 96, 114, 117
Market Street Burial Ground, 17, 26, 57
Mary Lyons School, 105

Wilson, President Woodrow, 111
Wilson, Rev. John, 3
Wilton Street, 86
Winship, Abiel, 31–33, 44–45
Winship, Charles, 31–32
Winship family, 13, 23–24, 33–35, 41, 55
Winship, Francis, 39
Winship Gardens, 39–40, 48
Winship, J. P. C., 31, 39, 72, 90, 93
Winship, Jonathan I, 22, 24, 29
Winship, Jonathan II, 22, 24, 31–32
Winship, Jonathan III, 32, 35, 39
Winship mansion (illus.), 23
Winship, Nathan, 33–34
Winship School, 44–45, 81
Winship Street, 59, 63, 110
Winship's Woods, 93
Winter Hill, 18
Winthrop, William, 30

Women's clubs in Brighton, 100–101, 111
Worcester, Dr. Noah, 39
Worcester Street, 62
Works Progress Administration (WPA), 116
World War I, 110–112
World War II, 118–119
WSBK-TV, 133

Y

Yale University, 58, 72
Yankee population, 100–104, 106–107, 109
York, Edythe, 135
Young Men's Christian Association (YMCA), 132

173

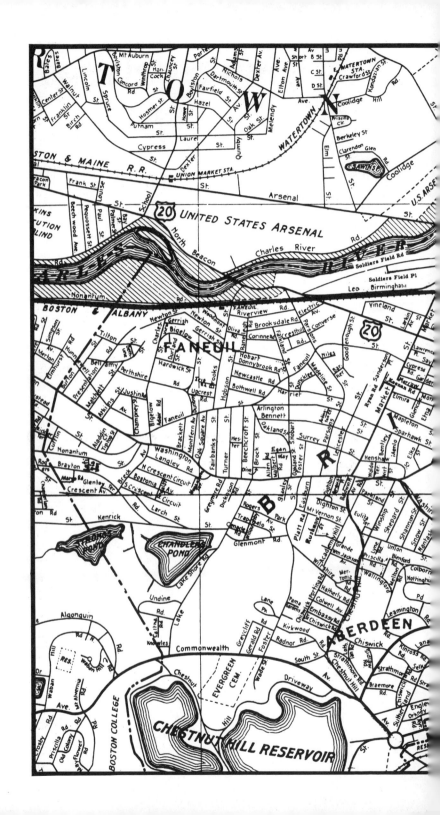

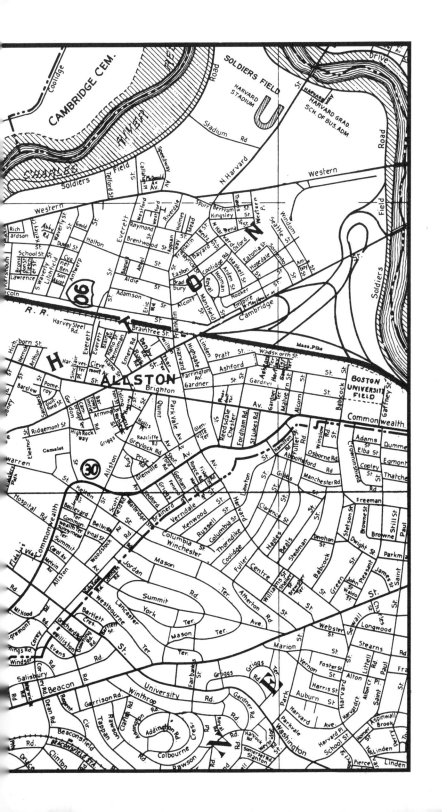

ABOUT THE AUTHOR

William P. Marchione was born and has lived in Brighton, Massachusetts all of his life. He is a graduate of Brighton High School, Boston University (A.B.), George Washington University (M.A.), and is currently working on a Ph.D. in urban history at Boston College. Marchione has taught American history in the Norwell, Massachusetts Public Schools since 1970. He served on the Boston School Committee in 1984 and 1985, representing the Allston-Brighton community. Articles by Marchione have appeared in the *New England Quarterly* and the *South Carolina Historical Magazine*. He has written and lectured widely on local history topics and is currently serving as President and Curator of the Brighton Historical Society.